UNITED STATES SECURITY ASSISTANCE

1977-1980: HUMAN RIGHTS ISSUES

AFFECTING ARMS TRANSFERS

I. Introduction

General Issue

Security assistance, the sale of arms, weaponry, and training to strengthen another nation in support of United States national interests, has long been an integral part of United States' foreign policy, with its most serious application beginning at the conclusion of World War II. Its importance to United States foreign policy execution is underscored by comments from former Secretary of State Henry A. Kissinger during an early 1970s speech about security assistance:

> Foreign policy must start with security. A nation's survival is its first and ultimate responsibility; it cannot be compromised or put to risk. There can be no security for us or others unless the strength of the free countries is in balance with that of potential adversaries, and no stability in power relationships is conceivable without America's active participation in world affairs. (DISAM:1-5)

Although a wealth of definitions have evolved over the years regarding security assistance, its statutory definition was outlined in the Foreign Assistance Act of 1961 and the Arms Export Control Act of 1976, both subsequently amended. These acts established programs by which the United States could provide defense articles, military training, and other defense related services, by grant, credit or cash sales, in furtherance of national policies and objectives. Forming a more basic viewpoint, former Secretary of State George F. Schultz stated in a 1983 address that "our security assistance program must be seen in the context of our national priority effort to establish the fact and capacity and <u>will</u> to build international peace, foster economic growth, and sustain mutual security" (DISAM:1-1). It is the aforementioned "reliability" and "will" which underscore the tremendous controversy surrounding the linkage of human rights issues with arms sales during the Carter Presidency.

Background

Against the backdrop of public dissent from the Vietnam conflict, widespread distrust of the presidency as a result of Watergate, and at a time when America was thirsting for change, James Earl Carter took the oath of office of the Presidency in 1977. As the first Democratic president in nearly a decade, one who ran for the presidency using an anti-Washington theme, President Carter embodied the hopes of many for a "new beginning" to national politics (Rozell:1). Determined to cleanse Washington of both the Watergate and Vietnam nightmares, he entered office proposing a multitude of sweeping reforms to national programs, one being the way the United States used security assistance as a tool of foreign policy. Within the security assistance program, President Carter set two lofty goals. First, he wanted to reduce the flow of arms globally by making arms transfers an "exceptional" foreign policy implement. Next, any security assistance provided would be linked to the recipient countries treatment of its populace. Although Congress had already addressed arms restraint and human rights issues within its passage of the Arms Export and Control Act of 1976, President Carter looked to take them one step further by simultaneously reducing arms transfers while also improving human rights treatment around the globe. Knowing full well any effort by the United States to restrict sales would require the willing support of friends and allies, President Carter emphasized its importance during one of his first speeches on the United States Conventional Arms Transfer Policy:

> I call upon suppliers and recipients alike to join us in a determined effort to make the world a safer place in which to live. (U.S. Congress, Committee on International Relations:175)

Sensing Americans were receptive to his assertions and reluctant to continue "business as usual" in Washington, President Carter proposed mass changes to the way security assistance was conducted, including the linking of security assistance based on that country's treatment of its populace. Where previous administrations overlooked these issues as determining factors, the Carter Administration attempted to convince the world of both the virtues of human rights and the benefits of arms restraint. Accordingly, no longer would human rights abuses be overlooked in favor of profit or peripheral national interests. This research will examine the Carter Security Assistance Program with special emphasis placed on the Carter human rights plan and his attempt to reduce the total number of conventional arms transfers.

Research Questions

This thesis will answer these research questions:

(1) Did the Carter Administration human rights agenda succeed in increasing awareness for human rights around the globe?;

(2) Was the program understood, was it implemented consistently, and what successes were achieved?

(3) Did the program contribute to a parallel goal of reducing the proliferation of arms around the globe?

Problem Statement

By examining the foundation, development, and execution of security assistance during the Carter Administration, this thesis will identify factors which influenced and limited the success of the Carter policy of arms restraint and the linking of security transfers to human rights issues. The desire of this research is to provide a better understanding of the plethora of complex interactions which impacted the security assistance program of the Carter administration.

Scope

This research follows the security assistance program from its post-World War II beginning in 1947 through the end of the Carter Administration in 1980. While a close look will be taken concerning legislative and real world events occurring during that time span, the primary focus will be on the arms restraint and human rights issues impacting security assistance as a decision-making tool of United States foreign policy from 1977 to 1980, the years Jimmy Carter was in office. Finally, in an effort to show the dramatic differences and the controversy surrounding the Carter security assistance program, the follow-on security assistance policies of President Reagan are examined.

Overview

This thesis consists of six chapters. Chapter one offers an introduction to the thesis subject and outlines the flow and direction of the research. Chapter two precisely describes and lists the methodology and variegated sources used to perform the research, along with establishing research limitations. Chapter three traces the development of security assistance over the past half century, summarizes security assistance legislation and peripheral issues over that same period, and examines the human rights movement of the early 70s. Chapter four contains the crucial determinations of factors which influenced security assistance during the Carter tenure as President, the heart of this research.

Chapter five provides a comparison of Carter policies with those of President Reagan when he took office. Significant changes between the two administration's are identified and examined, particularly in the treatment of human rights issues. Chapter six summarizes the report and offers conclusions with respect to the primary research questions.

II. Methodology

Chapter Overview

This chapter introduces the methodology used to collect and analyze data to solve my three research questions:

(1) Did the Carter Administration human rights agenda succeed in increasing the awareness for human rights around the globe?

(2) Was the program understood, was it implemented consistently, and what successes were achieved?

(3) Did the program contribute to a parallel goal of reducing the proliferation of arms around the globe?

Research Objectives

The objective of this research is to gain a better understanding of the factors which influenced the human rights policy of the Carter security assistance program. This research will examine the evolution, development, and implementation of the human rights agenda. First a general overview of the politics, legislation, and key determinants of security assistance will be presented flowing from the post-World War II Cold War beginnings up through the end of the Carter tenure. Next, a discussion of the human rights movement of the early 1970s will be presented with primary emphasis on its assimilation in the United States security assistance program. With the research having provided readers a background on the human rights revolution, the focus turns to President Carter and his attempt to meld arms restraint with human rights concerns during the 1977-1980 time period. Following this in-depth analysis, the research highlights the controversy surrounding the Carter security assistance program by examining changes made to security assistance after Ronald Reagan became President. Last and most importantly, an analysis will be conducted on the overall strategy behind the Carter directive of reducing arms and linking arms sales to human rights issues. By looking at all facets of the Carter plan, we will be able to analyze whether the Carter strategy fulfilled its dual objective of highlighting human rights issues while also stopping the proliferation of arms around the world. Furthermore, did it succeed in getting other countries to factor in human rights issues when contemplating and subsequently consummating the sale of arms to Third World Countries? What was the essence of the Carter strategy and why do historians point to it as a failed policy? These questions and others will be presented throughout this study in an attempt to examine the complex security assistance issues and their utilization during the late 1970s.

Research Design

For this study, an ex post facto design was utilized. This implies that there was no control over information gathered, and I could only report what happened during the Carter tenure in office (Cooper:141). This study relied exclusively on the use of historical research methodology which involved the process of collecting relevant historical data and examining their interrelationships (Dane:169). While many methods can be used to assess arms transfers, and this author does not pretend to have the qualifications nor expertise to perform an assessment on the military utility of transfers, I have accepted the multi-attributive utility theory advocated by Sherwin and Laurance which states, "human insight remains the most reliable means for synthesizing the interrelations among a complex set of international relations variables, and that one means of indexing an otherwise intangible concept is to tap the collective judgements of human experts (Sherwin and Laurance: 377).

My research is almost exclusively a cross-sectional study of the 1977-80 time period, but it will also be longitudinal in that I will compare pertinent studies accomplished during the early part of the Carter Administrations with similar ones completed after he left office. All data have been compared to ensure that information is accurate, and content is reliable and important.

Research Method

My research methodology consisted of data collection, comparative analysis of findings, and source documentation. Primary sources of data used to answer my research question relating to the formation and execution of the Carter security assistance program were as follows: legislation and legislative reports relating to foreign assistance; statistical records and reports of the Department of State and Defense and selected arms-related industry associations; executive orders and government regulations; memoirs from officials serving during the Carter Administration; previous thesis and doctoral studies; newspaper articles, periodical literature, and technical journals. Primary and secondary sources differ in that primary sources are original documents, eye witness accounts, and/or public records, while secondary sources are research studies performed by others offering an interpretation or contemporary view (Mozden:15). In this research the vast majority of data came from primary sources, with the secondary sources being previous thesis and doctoral studies on security assistance during the period in question. From this material I selected numerous articles, editorials, and commentaries that are representative of the general themes of these assessments. After collecting data from the aforementioned sources, I analyzed the findings for similarity and differences; weighed the reliability, validity, and accuracy; and factored out irrelevant data and data believed to be overly biased toward the subject.

Chapter Summary

The late 1970s offered the United States tremendous challenges in the way of implementing policy and transferring security assistance internationally. This chapter detailed the instruments used to perform my research on the United States Security Assistance Program during the Carter Administration. Ultimately, by reconstructing the political atmosphere prior to the Carter presidency, evaluating factors which permeated the Carter security assistance strategy, and performing a concise examination of the interrelated and opposing factors of security assistance, readers will be able arrive at conclusions which will be of some redeeming value in assessing past security assistance policies.

III. Literature Review

Chapter Overview

The objective of this chapter is to examine the evolution of the security assistance program for the purpose of providing background information critical to analyzing the security assistance program employed by President Carter and his administration. In tracing the development of the United States security assistance program, this chapter explores the evolution of security assistance; reviews legislation supporting our foreign policy objectives; looks at key ingredients contributing to the success of the program; and culminates with an overview of the human rights movement of the early 1970s. The chapter is divided into two main parts. The first part highlights the historical role of arms sales, focusing primarily on arms sales legislation and their use as a tool of foreign policy from 1947 to 1979. The remainder of the chapter examines the human rights movement, focusing primarily on the issues of the early 1970s.

Historical Role of Security Assistance

The first extensive use of arms sales in furtherance of United States interests occurred during WWI when approximately $2.2 billion in war supplies were extended to Europe (DISAM:1-13). After the war, the transfer of arms continued, reaching 52% of global arms exports by 1920. Alarmed by this escalation, Congress attempted to discourage arms transfers during the 1920s and early 1930s. To this end, a group of Senators known as the Nye Committee, conducted an investigation to determine the extent that arms manufacturers should be left to produce and sell weaponry without government intervention. This study transpired over a two year period, but little actually changed, except for an understanding that the government needed to keep closer tabs on arms control matters. This led the United States to retreat more toward its normal isolationist role (DISAM:1-14, 15). Stability prevailed until the late 30s when Mussolini's invasion of Abyssinia (1935), Hitler's invasion of the Rhineland (1936), and the start of the Spanish War (1937) put arms restraint on hold. In 1939, in conjunction with the escalating effects of World War II, the United States changed its "Neutrality Act" to allow for the sale of arms to Great Britain and selected other members of the allied nations on a cash-and-carry basis (DISAM:1-15). With traditional arms producers Britain and England focused on internal production, the United States enacted the Lend Lease Program on March 11, 1941, and earned the name "Arsenal of Democracy" (Sampson:87). The Lend Lease Program authorized the sale, exchange, lease, loan or other disposition of any defense article to any government deemed vital to U.S. defense interests. Deliveries under this program approximated nearly $49 billion by the conclusion of World War II (Hovey:182).

Security assistance increased as a national security tool at the conclusion of World War II to combat the exploitation of Europe and Asia by the Soviet Union. From the onset of the postwar period, American policymakers confronted the impossible task of reconstructing a world order shattered by three decades of global war, economic dislocation, depression, and political and social revolution (Nathan:9). Much discussion has taken place concerning the United States involvement during the post-WWII period and two primary theories have surfaced. The first, an "orthodox" view, contends that American foreign policy responses are defensive reactions to Soviet Union communist "expansionism." The second view, termed a "revisionists" perspective, places most of the blame for the Cold War on United States capitalism and the need to secure markets, raw materials, and cheap labor (Nathan:6). Regardless of which theory one believes, the prevailing approach of the United States Government has been to use arms transfers as a major instrument of foreign policy.

Arms transfers increased markedly in the 1950s, but the low level of sales (under $500 million per year) had little impact on the economy, as few nations could afford to purchase equipment. With the establishment of more competitive pricing policies and the long-awaited economic recovery of several European nations, sales began to grow by the early 1960s (Hovey:83-5). This trend remained constant until 1968 when arms sales to Third World countries actually surpassed sales to First World countries (Pierre:12). After 1968, arms sales remained high until the end of the Vietnam conflict. After the Vietnam conflict, both Congress and the American public wanted to change the manner by which the United States conducted its foreign policy and more specifically, its security assistance program.

Arms Sale Legislation and Key Events

Truman Doctrine. Resulting from ever increasing hostility from the Soviet Union, one of our World War II allies, the United States enacted specific legislation to "contain" this new foe. In response to the Soviet's seizure of several small East European countries and the issuing of threats to Turkey, the U.S. drafted the Truman Doctrine. The cornerstone of the "containment" of Soviet expansionism after World War II, and the seeds behind the subsequent Cold War, a speech by President Truman to Congress on March 12, 1947, claimed the virtues of providing American assistance to countries threatened by the Soviet Union. In his speech, President Truman stated that the United States must adhere to a policy of supporting free people who are resisting subjugation by armed minorities or by outside pressures (Graves:4). Furthermore, he declared:

> I believe that we must assist free peoples to work out their own destinies in their own way.
>
> I believe that our help should be primarily through economic and financial aid which is essential to economic stability and orderly political processes.

This legislation proved to be the genesis behind the U.S. security assistance program and became known as the Truman Doctrine. Closely following this legislation was the passing of the Greek-Turkish Aid Bill of 1947.

Greek-Turkish Aid Bill. Referred to often in the same context as the Truman Doctrine, the Greek-Turkish Aid Bill established the first post-World War II major commitment by the United States to a foreign country (Graves:183). Recognized as the building block of later security assistance programs, this bill earmarked $400 million for a program of military and economic support for Greece and Turkey (Hutchins:6) The aid to Turkey helped counter Soviet attempts to gain control of the Dardanelles, the Soviet's escape route into the Mediterranean Sea. The "Dardanelles issue" became a problem when Soviet leadership contacted Turkey and proposed a new common ownership which would exclude all nations except for the Black Sea powers (Truman:96). Fortunately, after consulting with the United States, Turkey decided to resist the Soviet thrust, but laid an enormous burden upon the United States for financial assistance to continue the resistance path, saying "The burden is too great for the nation's economy to carry much longer" (Truman: 98).

The situation in Greece was also linked to the Dardanelles and was the direct result of Soviet support of Communist guerrilla activity on the Greek-Albanian border (Truman: 98). This was recognized as an attempt by the Soviet Union to gain power in Greece and further the possibility of dominating the vital sea lane from the Mediterranean through the Suez Canal (Curti:771). Of importance to the evolving United States security assistance program, the original supporter of Greek forces, Great Britain, announced in February of 1947 that it could no longer provide military and economic support to Greece (Hovey:4). The biggest concern to the United States was that Greece would fall into Soviet hands if not backed financially which would result in Turkey being surrounded by Communism

(Truman:100). After meeting with a joint session of Congress, President Truman recommended that the United States provide immediate support (Hovey:5). Although the American public was initially unresponsive to this request for fear that the United States was unnecessarily interfering in the internal affairs of another nation, the Senate eventually approved the legislation on April 22, 1947 and the House approved in early May (Truman:108). As mentioned earlier, this became known as the Truman Doctrine and marked the beginning of the United States' policy of Soviet containment.

Marshall Plan. Following passage of the Greek-Turkish aid program, the focus turned to providing economic assistance to the rest of war-torn Europe. The revitalization of Europe was critical to the United States in achieving its primary objective of checking Soviet "expansionist" moves upon a vulnerable Europe. To help facilitate this objective, a comprehensive economic aid package, named the Marshall Plan[1] (after Secretary of State George C. Marshall), committed the United States to supplying billions of dollars to recipients in Western Europe to accelerate their economic recovery. Three different approaches surfaced during congressional hearings (Arkes:137). The first plan was referred to as "actions on the level of political institutions." One proponent of this plan, Senator William Fulbright, urged an explicit commitment to European political interaction--in essence, a United States of Europe (Arkes:138). Fearing among other things that a philosophy tying United States in Europe would be interpreted as political intervention, Senator Alben Barkley argued that it was not the United States' responsibility, nor did it have the constitutional authority to create a political unification act (Arkes:138). Thus, after substantial opposition mounted, the issue of political unification of Europe was defeated in 1949 and failed to reach conference in 1950.

---

[1] Also referred to as the Economic Cooperation Act of 1948.

The second approach, referred to as "covert, organizational incentives," although not as radical as the first plan, also had shortcomings. Viewed as another attempt to place American influence in Europe, the plan, devised by Senator Charles Taft, created a position for a special representative in Europe. Through establishing this position, U.S. representatives hoped to keep it separate from the Marshall Plan and avoid denouncement by the Soviets as an imperialistic move (Arkes:139). After much debate, an Office of the Special Representative (OSR) was created in Paris to centralize and streamline United States' European operations. Illustrating the growing emphasis of this operation, the number of staff personnel assigned grew from between 30 and 40 specialists in 1948, to 1,455 by 1953 (Arkes:140).

The final approach, termed "incentives of administrative power," was an attempt to link European aid as a single unit, rather than separate it by country. This idea was rejected due to problems in defining meaningful enforcement conditions, and the impossible task of monitoring and disciplining disruptive members (Arkes:141).

Among the many things troubling the total economic recovery of Europe were three important agendas: (1) just distribution of resources to European countries; (2) keeping some degree of fairness in helping the recovery of Germany; and (3) appeasing the British, who sternly opposed most of the plan (Arkes:142). Despite the wealth of concerns put forth by its benefactors, the Marshall Plan did succeed in dispersing $12.5 billion in aid to participating nations (DISAM:3-21).

NATO. Concluding that economic assistance by itself could not stem Soviet expansionist thrusts in Europe, the United States agreed to join an association with Europe on April 4, 1949, called the North Atlantic Treaty Organization (NATO). Ratification of this agreement with eleven other European nations was approved by a Senate vote of 83 - 13 (Arkes:144). Signed by representatives of Belgium, Canada, Denmark, France, Iceland, Italy, Luxembourg, the Netherlands, Norway, Portugal, the

United Kingdom, and the United States, the agreement stated that an attack against one was an attack against all (House, 1949:44). NATO was established to provide the primary defense against communist aggression in Europe through its political/military infrastructure (DISAM:1-19). With the establishment of missile bases, deployment of nuclear weapons, basing rights, and the rebuilding and restructuring of West Germany, NATO has withstood many tests of will put forth by communist-inspired regimes.

Mutual Defense Assistance Act of 1949. In 1949, following the creation of NATO, the U.S. passed the Mutual Defense Assistance Act (MDAA), an act which placed the U.S. in the center of collective security for noncommunist countries and created authority for foreign military assistance. By passing the act, the U.S. sent a clear message that U.S. efforts to promote peace and stability were based on the principle of "continuous and effective self-help and mutual aid" (Graves:10). Because of this act, the President maintained a large degree of flexibility in establishing agreements with countries to safeguard the interests of the United States and its allies. The MDAA provided $500,000,000 in military support to NATO countries, and a lesser amount to support Greece, Turkey, Iran, Korea, and the Philippines (House:1949, 28-29). Initial assistance, in the form of material, technical assistance, and manufacturing/tooling, allowed Europe to increase its own production of military items without seriously interfering with its economic recovery (Edwards:16).

Mutual Security Act of 1951. The act addressed how security assistance would be used to maintain United States foreign policy by providing military, technical, and economic assistance to friendly countries. Moreover, this act achieved better control over foreign aid programs by consolidating them under one program. This reorganization of assistance strengthened the collective defense of the Free World and further promoted the national interests of the United States.

Mutual Security Act of 1954. In 1954 Congress passed the third major security assistance legislation, the Mutual Security Act. This act repealed fourteen pieces of legislation and consolidated them into one bill, simplifying the purpose and direction of U.S. foreign aid (Edwards:21). In the midst of closer congressional scrutiny, this act stood as the benchmark of security assistance until 1961, when the Foreign Assistance Act was approved.

Foreign Assistance Act (FAA) of 1961. This act transformed U.S. foreign assistance from a short-range to a long-range program and consolidated economic aid, military assistance, and sales under a single statute. The purpose of the FAA of 1961 was to promote the foreign policy, security, and general welfare of the United States by assisting peoples of the world in their efforts toward economic development and internal and external security (FAA of 1961).

This FAA of 1961 empowered the President to authorize military assistance to friendly countries if it would promote world peace and/or strengthen the security of the United States. It also afforded presidential flexibility in obtaining defense articles from any source and loaning, giving, or selling the articles to selected nations. Whereas the Mutual Security Act of 1954 permitted a 3-year credit period, the FAA of 1961 emphasized the principle of continuity, with development loans repayable on manageable terms with emphasis on long-term financing (Senate, miscellaneous reports:1). All loans made to eligible countries were based on a 50-year repay, with interest rates as low as 1 percent and in certain cases, no repayment of principal for periods up to 10 years (Senate Misc:10). The maximum value of defense articles granted to any single country was limited to $3 million annually, but this restriction was waived if the President determined it was prudent and in the best interests of strengthening the Free World.

Along with legislative changes, Secretary of Defense McNamara created the Office of International Logistics Negotiations to actively promote the sale of military equipment abroad (Feigl:2). McNamera stated, "I should like to encourage sales of military equipment appropriate to meet the needs of foreign nations in every possible way (Feigl:5)." According to McNamera, the objective of the sales were to:

(1) Promote the defensive strength of our allies, consistent with our political-economic objectives

(2) Promote the concept of cooperative logistics and standardization with our allies.

(3) Offset the unfavorable balance of payments resulting from essential U.S. military deployment abroad. (Feigl:5)

The FAA of 1961 also prescribed eligibility conditions which needed to be certified by the President before military assistance could be provided. The conditions stipulated by the legislation were:

(1) material would only be used for the purpose originally provided;

(2) material would not be transferred without U.S. permission;

(3) recipients were to permit continuous observation of the use of the items by representatives of the U.S. Government; and

(4) recipients were required to return to the U.S. any articles no longer needed for the purposes originally supplied. (DISAM:23-3)

Additionally, the FAA of 1961 stated that assistance would not be provided to any country that is communist controlled; seizes, nationalizes, or expropriates U.S. property; and/or engages in aggressive military acts against the U.S. or other countries receiving U.S. aid (DISAM:23-3).

From the time of its origination in 1961 until the Arms Export Control Act of 1976, the FAA underwent numerous revisions. Revisions included: reduction or elimination of all grant aid to any country having sufficient wealth that it could maintain and equip its own military (U.S. Congress, Joint Committee:75); prohibitions against furnishing assistance to any country giving assistance to Cuba[2]; and prohibitions against providing assistance to any country which seizes, or imposes penalty or sanction against, any United States fishing vessel on account of its fishing activities in international waters (U.S. Congress, Joint Committee:104). Other noteworthy provisions included prohibitions against any country permitting its aircraft or ships to transport cargo to North Vietnam and Cuba[3] (US Congress, Joint Committee:104); restrictions on assistance to countries permitting or failing to prevent mob action against U.S. property; and the requirement (1969) for the number of foreign students trained in the United States to be equal or less than the number or foreign civilians brought to the U.S. in the preceding year (U.S. Congress, Joint Committee:79). A later amendment to the FAA of 1961[4] included a human rights section. In it Congress declared:

> It is the sense of Congress that, except in extraordinary circumstances, the President shall substantially reduce or terminate security assistance to any government which engages in a consistent pattern of gross violations of internationally recognized human rights, including torture or cruel, inhuman or degrading treatment or punishment; prolonged detention without charges; or other flagrant denials of the right to life, liberty, and the security of the person. (U.S. Congress, Joint Committee:69)

Foreign Military Sales Act of 1968. In the midst of ever-growing anti-war sentiment over the U.S. war effort in Vietnam, and tremendous opposition from Congress, President Lyndon Johnson steadfastly attempted to maintain the level of American foreign aid. Because of President Johnson's opposition to congressional efforts to decrease foreign aid, Congress passed the Foreign Military Sales Act. This allowed Congress to place added controls and prohibitions on weapons sales, amending the Foreign Military

---

[2] This restriction could be waived if it was deemed in the national interest of the U.S.
[3] This could also be waived by the President if in his judgement it was in the best interests of the United States
[4] Incorporated in 1974.

Sales Act of 1961 (U.S. Congress, Foreign Military Sales Act:preamble). Congress also restricted Export-Import Bank loans to developed countries, placed stringent controls and ceilings on foreign military sales (U.S. Congress, Foreign Military Sales Act:2761-4), and authorized the sale of defense equipment to friendly nations wealthy enough to sustain their own military forces and to whom the sale would inevitably bolster in some sense the security objectives of the United States. The intent of the toughened legislation was to stem the flow of security assistance which had exceeded $3 billion from 1965 to 1967 (Divine:84). The rationalization behind this approach is found in the following passage:

> It is the sense of the Congress that all such sales be approved only when they are consistent with the foreign policy interests of the United States, the purposes of the foreign assistance program of the United States as embodied in the Foreign Assistance Act of 1961, . . . the extent and character of the military requirement, and the economic and financial capability of the recipient country. (U.S. Congress, Foreign Military Sales Act:Sec.1)

Because of the increased scrutiny of foreign aid and the resultant congressional upheaval, the Foreign Military Sales (FMS) Act of 1968 was approved. This act divided foreign military sales into two separate categories, cash and credit, and revised and consolidated all foreign assistance legislation related to military exports. Sales were approved only if they were consistent with existing American foreign policy practices and interests (U.S. At Large:1320). It was stipulated that the sale had to contribute to the security of the U.S., and the receiving country would not be allowed to transfer the articles to any nation without U.S. approval.

International Security Assistance and Arms Export Control Act of 1976. Recognizing a need to change the structure of foreign aid, Congress passed the International Security Assistance and Arms Export Control Act of 1976. This act amended the Foreign Assistance Act of 1961, created the Arms Export Control Act (AECA), and established provisions for the International Military Education and Training

(IMET) Program. The AECA consolidated and completely revised arms export laws and was passed in an effort to check the President's ability to sell arms at will (Joiner:243). The AECA reflected a policy change from arms sales to arms control and gave Congress the power to veto proposed arms sales. It also significantly changed the arms sales structure, in effect realigning and reversing the power base which previously had afforded the executive branch complete control over arms trading policy (US Congress, Senate: Committee on Foreign Relations, International Security Assistance and Arms Export Act of 1976-1977:8-15). The act also gave Congress more time to debate the merits of legislation, extending the period of time allowed to veto sales from twenty to thirty days (Labrie:9-10). Despite the serious revision of power from the Executive Branch to Congress, the President still possessed the power to veto congressional review if he felt the national security of the United States was in jeopardy.

International Security Assistance Act of 1979. Beset by concerns that countries were still receiving security assistance while allegedly practicing human rights violations, the International Security Assistance Act of 1979 was passed, setting forth guidelines in regard to human rights:

> In allocating the funds authorized to be appropriated by this Act and the Arms Export Control Act, the President shall take into account significant improvements in the human rights records of recipient countries, except that such allocations may not contravene any other provisions of law. (U.S. Congress, International Security Assistance Act of 1979:702)

This law was passed in an effort to reduce the dollar amount of U.S. commitments in the area of arms sales. The Act prohibited aid to Angola, Zambia, Tanzia, and Mozambique because of their involvement in the troubled region of southern Africa; allowed for a matching of funds for the IMET Program at its 1979 level of $31,800,000; and called for a reduction in spending on peace-keeping operations in the amount of $9,800,000 (U.S. Congress, International Assistance Act of 1979:705).

The emphasis of this research now shifts to miscellaneous important factors which impact the United States' Security Assistance Program, first looking at the major components of the program.

U.S. Security Assistance Program Components

Military Assistance Program (MAP).[5] MAP, a program stemming from the MDAA and created in 1949, made it legal to loan or grant (the normal practice) military equipment, materials, and services to eligible nations. Most often this DOD transaction, was made to U.S. allies "free of charge" (DISAM:1-17). With the addition of the MAP, arms transfers, economic aid, and collective security emerged under the umbrella of security assistance. From FY 1950 - FY 1982, the United States expended over $54 billion to foreign countries through our military assistance/grant aid programs (DISAM:2-11).

Authorized by the Foreign Assistance Act of 1976, the act serves as the vehicle by which the United States provides training in the United States and selected foreign countries to foreign military and civilian personnel, and like MAP, is on a grant basis. The objective of the IMET is improved readiness; standardization of weapons and doctrine; and increased access to future key military personnel and leaders of foreign countries (DISAM:2-12).

The Economic Support Fund (ESF). Authorized by Chapter 4, Part II of the Foreign Assistance Act, the ESF was established to promote economic and political stability in special interest areas to secure peace and/or avert major crises. ESF provides

---

[5] In reviewing the period under review for this study, MAP is listed as one of the major components although in FY 1990 MAP was formally merged with the Foreign Military Financing Program (FMFP) to integrate MAP funding into the appropriations account for the FMF Program.

balance of payment support, and infrastructure and technical assistance development project support and is administered by the Agency for International Development. Additional program support is available to assist in health, education, agriculture, and family planning development projects.

Peacekeeping Operations (PKO). Authorized by Chapter 6, Part II of the Foreign Assistance Act, this security assistance component provides for the share of security assistance programmed for the Multinational Force and Observers (MFO), U.S. forces operating under the United Nations Forces in Cyprus (UNFCYP), and any of a number of places around the globe requiring U.S. support.

The FMS and Foreign Military Construction Sales Financing Program. Authorized under provisions of the AECA, this nonappropriated program provides the U.S. the capability to extend credit and loan repayment guarantees to foreign governments to purchase defense articles, services, and training. Under this arrangement, the purchasing government pays all applicable sales costs and the military articles and services may be provided from DOD stocks or via new procurement.

Foreign Military Construction Sales involve the sale of design and construction services to approved purchasers and closely resemble those of the FMS Program.

Commercial Sales Licensed Under the AECA. Authorized under Section 38 of the AECA, this sale is made by the U.S. industry directly to a foreign buyer. This transaction is not administered by the DOD and does not involve an agreement with another country, although the selling company must obtain a license from the Department of State. Sales of this type are governed by the International Traffic in Arms Regulations (ITAR).

Human Rights Background

The issue of human rights has been around as long as man himself, but in this century came to the forefront during World War II after reports of the holocaust. Following World War II, the push for human rights escalated within the United Nations and according to author Theo C. Van Boven in his work "The United Nations and Human Rights: A Critical Appraisal (Rubin:19)," can be divided into three separate decades. While this research will not discuss each period in detail, it is nonetheless important to explain the three periods. The first decade (1945-1955) is referred to as the stage of standard-setting, the second decade (1955-1965), the stage of promotion, and (1965-1975), the stage of protection. Though this distinction is not perfect in the sense that only one phase was being accomplished at a time, it is still important when one tries to grasp the vast changes the world has undergone over that span.

During the standard-setting phase, the Universal Declaration of Human Rights was passed. With President Truman serving as the United Nations self-proclaimed spokesman, he and the United Nations' Commission on Human Rights were tasked with laying down the foundation for the aforementioned Universal Declaration of Human Rights. The Declaration was consummated on 10 December 1948 and as the human rights standard-bearer, has been referred to endless times at the national and international level during discussions on human rights concerns. The Declaration was important in that it stated that human rights and freedoms were not related to "race, color, sex, language, religion, political or other opinion, national or social origin, property, birth or other status (Pollis:4)." The Declaration also enumerated the rights and freedom articles of life, liberty, the illegality of torture, equality before the law, prohibition against arbitrary arrest, fair trial by impartial tribunal, the right to be presumed innocent until proven guilty, freedom of travel, the right to marry freely, the right to own property, freedom of assembly, and so on (Pollis:5).

The effort by the United Nations was important in that it established a foundation by which governments could argue human rights issues. And there were a plenitude of human rights issues from 1945-1975. Some of the more obvious ones involved human rights issues in southern Africa, Portugal, Namibia, and Rhodesia (Boven:374-393). Other areas where the United Nations queried about human rights included the Middle East, and Chile. Unfortunately, the majority of time any information gathered by the United Nations was secondary as representatives were almost never allowed to enter and scrutinize the country in question. Additionally, the procedures by which the United Nations got involved were laden with procedural technicalities and time-consuming. These difficulties led to many disappointments and it became obvious that despite all the high expectations within the United Nations, the organization was not the quintessential solution to human rights problems as it lacked authority to take necessary action. Thus, for the most part, the suffering of individuals within abusing countries continued unabated.

The United Nations was not the only organization where human rights were being addressed. In 1949, the Consultative Assembly took up proposals for a European Convention on human rights (Gordon:804). Taking many of the tenets of the Universal Declaration, the Convention established eleven rights as subjects for protection (Council:102-106).

1. The right to life

2. Freedom from torture, inhuman or degrading treatment

3. Freedom from slavery or servitude

4. The right to individual liberty

5. The right to a fair trial

6. Prohibition of ex post facto criminal legislation

7. Respect for private and family life

8. Freedom of thought, conscience and religion

9. Freedom of expression

10. Freedom of peaceful assembly and association

11. The right to marry and found a family

In addition to the listed rights, the Convention also set forth rights regarding the right to property, education, and free elections in the First Additional Protocol to the Convention[6]. Other protocols protected freedom of movement, and prohibition against imprisonment for failure to fulfill a contract. In many ways the Convention possesses more power than the United Nations because it has remedies for people believing himself or herself to be the victim of a human rights violation by a state party to the Convention. This marked one of the few times an individual was granted legal standing before a supranational tribunal (Hudson:35-70).

The European human rights system was founded with two primary levels. The first level deals with what are termed "routine" allegations, while the second naturally involves more serious violations. In the states of Austria, Belgium, and the United Kingdom, the system is taken so seriously that victims of human rights violations have been paid compensation.

Following in the footsteps and in many ways an expansion of the civil rights movement of the 1960s, the issue of universal human rights in the United States came to the forefront in the early 1970s as Congress began to aggressively study human rights conditions in countries receiving U.S. aid. Additional impetus for human rights policies was created because of the intensive backlash from our Vietnam involvement and the growing distrust of our Executive office resulting from Watergate.

---

[6] Ratified by Austria, Belgium, Cyprus, Denmark, France, the Federal Republic of Germany, Greece, Iceland, Ireland, Italy, Luxembourg, Malta, the Netherlands, Norway, Portugal, Sweden, Switzerland, Turkey, and the United Kingdom.

When exactly did this movement start in Congress? In 1973, an amendment was introduced by Senator James Abourezk[7] which stated congressional beliefs that the Executive office should deny economic or military assistance to governments which intern or imprison its citizens for political purposes (Brown:7) Following this, Senator Edward Kennedy introduced the first amendment related to human rights abuses. The amendment, dealing with abuses in Chile, was not punitive but expressed Congress' belief that Chile should make an effort to improve its human rights track record. This emphasis continued throughout 1973, as the House Subcommittee on International Organizations and Movements held 15 hearings and constructed a report titled *Human Rights in the World Community: A Call for U.S. Leadership* (Brown:xvi). In this report, Congress called for the State Department to treat issues regarding human rights practices consistently across the board regardless of whether the government in question was friendly, neutral, or unfriendly. The report also identified acceptable methods by which the U.S. could intervene on the behalf of improving human rights practices. The four methods advocated in this report included: "private consultations with governments alleged to be in violation of global human rights treatment; public intervention by way of United Nations' agencies; reduction or elimination of military assistance; and/or withdrawal of certain economic assistance programs.

One manner by which Congress aggressively used its power was in passing human rights amendments to foreign assistance bills. Liberals and conservatives alike supported the concept of linking foreign assistance programs to the level of respect for human rights in recipient countries. Critics viewed this as another ill-advised attempt by the U.S. to conform the world to its moralistic will, as well as justification for cutting back on security assistance.

---

[7] This became Section 32 of the Foreign Assistance Act of 1973.

The push for human rights continued in 1974 as legislators established a human rights office in the State Department and set up a series of laws and resolutions which made certain U.S. aid programs subject to human rights conditions. Also, a provision to limit the ceiling on security assistance provided for South Korea was adopted and could be exceeded only if Korea made substantial progress in the observance of internationally recognized standards of human rights (U.S. Congress, Foreign Assistance Act of 1974:section 26). This marked the first time under the new policy that economic assistance was limited. Later in 1974, an amendment in Section 502B applied to all countries receiving security assistance. This provision defined violation by countries as follows:

> Any country which engages in a consistent patter of gross violations of internationally recognized human rights, including torture or cruel, inhuman, or degrading treatment or punishment, prolonged detention without charges, or other flagrant denial of the right to life, liberty, and the security of the person. (U.S. Congress, Foreign Assistance Act of 1974:Section 502B)

The human rights crusade extended into other areas as well. The Jackson-Vanik amendment linked trade preferences of "nonmarket economy" countries with its emigration policies and linked human rights conditions within the United States détente[8] structure (Brown:6). An effort was made to go beyond the words of human rights policies as section 116, modeled on section 502B was enacted, and affected all bilateral economic assistance (Brown:7). This mandatory provision cited that,

> "No assistance may be provided under this part to the government of any country which engages in a consistent pattern of gross violations of internationally recognized human rights, including torture or cruel, inhuman, degrading treatment or punishment, prolonged detention without charges, or other flagrant denial of the right to life, liberty, and the security of the person, unless such assistance will directly benefit the needy people in such country. (Brown:8)

---

[8] A process by which two or more nations move away from a continuous confrontation with each other in the general direction of cooperation.

This definition meant that countries in violation of human rights could still receive aid if it was assessed that the needy would still reap the benefits of other types of aid.

Emphasis on human rights did not subside in 1975 or 1976. In 1975, Congressman Tom Harkin introduced legislation which affected loans granted by the Inter-American Development and African Development Banks. The provision directed the secretary of the treasury to instruct U.S. delegates to those banks to vote against loans on the basis of consistent patterns of violations, although like other similar legislation, loopholes were provided for aid benefiting the needy. The most stinging legislation occurred in 1976 when full and complete reports were mandated on human rights conditions in countries receiving security assistance. These reports would serve as decision-making tools for security assistance approval unless extraordinary circumstances justified continuing aid under existing conditions.

By 1983 there were fifty-four specific pieces of legislation involving human rights issues (Mower:62). The categories impacted by this human rights movement included, the FAA of 1961 as amended, the AECA, the Agricultural Trade Development and Assistance Act of 1954 as amended, legislation dealing with international financing institutions, the Bretton Woods Agreement Act as amended, the Export-Import Bank Act of 1945 as amended, the Trade Act of 1974, State Department Acts of 1982 and 1983, Foreign Relations Authorization Act 1979, and country specific provisions relating to twelve nations (Mower:62). At a minimum, the U.S. effort had brought human rights concerns, at least temporarily, to the forefront.

Human Rights Definition

Extensive research has been conducted on human rights and although no definition is accepted by all, certain inalienable issues are found in most all definitions.

The four most often mentioned are: (1) all persons have them; (2) all persons share them equally, (3) they do not depend on any special status or relations; and (4) they can be claimed from or asserted against the actions of any and all other humans and institutions (Brown:xix).

How are they (human rights) prioritized? Under Carter's leadership there were two agencies primarily responsible for overseeing human rights issues. There was the House Subcommittee on International Organizations, and the Office of the Assistant Secretary for Human Rights and Humanitarian Affairs (Brown xxiii). These agencies gathered and studied information on human rights conditions in recipient countries and reported their findings to Congress. As previously discussed, countries determined to have exceeded the threshold on human rights abuses were cut off from aid unless "extraordinary" circumstances justified continuing the aid inspite of the human rights abuse citing.

What strategies are acceptable by the U.S. government in promoting human rights in conjunction with foreign policy? Many strategies have been proposed, but one repeating theme is that any strategy involving human rights policies should be flexible rather than setting one universal standard. This supports the idea put forth by some who say that our national interests are ultimately more important than human rights concerns. This explains why Congress incorporates loopholes in many of its policies to allow "national interest" concerns to supersede human rights issues in selected cases. During the Carter tenure, these loopholes enabled the U.S. to supply an abundance of arms to the repressive governments of Iran, the Philippines, and South Korea.

Helsinki Conference

On August 1, 1975, at the conclusion of a historic three-day meeting in Helsinki, Finland, the leaders of 35 Eastern and Western European countries, plus the U.S. and Canada, signed the final act of the conference on Security and Cooperation in Europe. This culminated more than two years of negotiations on declared goals of "peace, security, justice and cooperation. The final act was produced in six official languages[9] and was comprised of four sections covering a variety of security, economic, cooperation and human rights issues. Although the conference had its merits, the meetings two biggest participants, the United States and the Soviet Union, differed measurably in their views on human rights and internal affairs. Soviet President Leonid Brezhnev's official statement of July 31, 1975 underscores the dramatic differences between the Soviet position and that of the United States.

> No one should try to dictate to other peoples on the basis of foreign policy considerations of one kind or another the manner in which they ought to manage their internal affairs. It is only the people of each given state, and no one else, who have the sovereign right to resolve their internal affairs and establish their internal laws. A different approach would be perilous as a ground for international cooperation. (Maresca:130)

Despite the stark difference between the conference's two main participants, the lengthy negotiation process did culminate in establishing a foundation for human rights debate between countries differing in customs, traditions, and history. Excepts from the treaty pertaining to human rights:

> The participating states will respect human rights and fundamental freedoms, including the freedom of thought, conscience, religion or belief, for all without distinction as to race, sex, language or religion.

---

[9] English, French, German, Russian, Italian, and Spanish.

They will promote and encourage the effective exercise of civil, political, economic, social, cultural and other rights and freedoms all of which derive from the inherent dignity of the human person and are essential for his free and full development.

Within this framework the participating states will recognize and respect the freedom of the individual to profess and practice, alone or in a community with others, religious or belief acting in accordance with the dictates of his own conscience.

The participating states on whose territory national minorities exist will respect the right of persons belonging to such minorities to equality before the law, will afford them the full opportunity for the actual employment of human rights and fundamental freedoms and will, in this manner, protect their legitimate interests in this sphere.

The participating states recognize the universal significance of human rights and fundamental freedoms, respect for which is an essential factor for the peace, justice and well-being necessary to insure the development of friendly relations and cooperation among themselves as among all states.

They will constantly respect these rights and freedoms in their mutual relations and will endeavor jointly and separately, including in co-operation with the United Nations, to promote universal and effect respect for them.

They confirm the right of the individual to know and act upon his rights and duties in this field.

In the field of human rights and fundamental freedoms, the participating states will act in conformity with the purposes and principles of the Charter of the United Nations and with the Universal Declaration of Human Rights. They will also fulfill their obligations as set forth in the international declarations and agreements in this field, including inter alia the International Covenants on Human Rights, by which they may be bound. (Facts:11-17)

The difficulty of merging Western views on human rights with those of Easterners and the rest of the world is reflected in the two years it took to complete the Helsinki treaty. Who benefited most from the Helsinki Conference? This is a difficult question to answer as the following 1975 editorial from the Oregon Journal suggests:

The question of "who won?" at Helsinki will be argued interminably. It may not be answered for another 10 to 20 years.

Critics, particularly in the United States, say that the West gave away too much, since the 30,000-word joint declaration, signed by the leaders of 35 nations, recognizes Soviet World War II territorial gains. Defenders respond that the statement, which is not a treaty, does no such thing. At worst, it does not "give away" anything that had not been won 30 years ago, which the West has no conceivable intention of trying to change by force.

Realistically, the Helsinki meeting was only a way station on the long, long road toward trying to reduce the danger of mutual destruction by nuclear war. It won't have served its purpose if there is not steady continuation of efforts, through SALT and Mutual Balanced Force Reduction (MBFR) negotiations to cut back on the arms race.

The alternative is an endless, costly spiral in the development of ever more destructive weapons and the increasing danger that they will be used on a scale that would spell the end of civilization. The most hopeful side of the Helsinki agreement lies admittedly in the intangibles, the contents of what is labeled "Basket Three," wherein freer exchange of information and greater human contacts between East and West are espoused.

There is no means of enforcing these provisions, but they were resisted at first by the Soviet Union, and in arguing for them, Western negotiators were sometimes joined by spokesman from Eastern bloc nations. It is reported that negotiations included some "behind-the-scene scrapping" between the Russians and their client states. Time magazine quotes a Dutch participant as having said: "The Soviets have never been so clobbered before by their satellites, and that's bound to leave a mark."

It is a matter of opinion whether the Helsinki pact weakened the Brezhnev Doctrine, which sought to give Moscow control over the Eastern bloc. If the words of Soviet Leader Leonid Brezhnev at Helsinki could be taken at face value, that would be the case, for he said that "no one should try to dictate to other peoples. . . the manner in which they ought to manage their internal affairs."

The Soviet boss may not have been thinking of Czechoslovakia, East Germany or Romania when he uttered the words, but a lot of other people did, including many in those countries. The self-righteousness which condemns the Helsinki pact is similar to the attitude which got us into the Vietnam quagmire. Vietnam taught us to be more realistic about the world.

The strategy now is to hold on to our principles, keep our guard up and work for peaceful change. In a world living with a mutual balance of terror, what alternative do we have? (Facts:23)

Chapter Summary

This chapter served three primary purposes. First it provided a recap of the politics and legislation which surrounded the United States security assistance program from its post-World War II roots up through discussion of the International Security Assistance Act of 1979. Next, the six primary methods by which the United States extends security assistance to perspective recipients were examined. Finally, human rights were discussed. This section consisted of two distinctive parts. The first part reviewed the history behind human rights issues while the final part examined human rights issues permeating the United States from the early 1970s until President Carter arrived in office.

IV. Background of Carter Security Assistance Program

Chapter Overview

The objective of this chapter is to review the major components of President Carter's security assistance program, discuss problems with defining and implementing his human rights policy, and provide a framework for the critical assessment of his administration's effectiveness in merging arms restraint and human rights policies with the security assistance aspect of U.S. foreign policy. President Carter's performance will be assessed according to:

1. The degree to the human rights policy succeeded in increasing awareness for human rights around the globe.

2. The degree to which the policy was implemented consistently.

3. The degree to which Presidential Directive 13 helped reduce the proliferation of arms around the globe?

Campaign Strategy

Any study dealing with President Carter's security assistance policies would not be complete without looking closely at the foundation of the human rights aspect of his program. Entering the presidential race as a relative unknown and advocating what some refer to as a "rookie" position in politics, evidence points to Carter being more ideological than political. As one of the driving points of his campaign and the primary focus of this research, the evolution of the human rights issue happened more by accident than design. Although there is little doubt Carter fostered hope that all people would be treated with respect and dignity, that this issue was an original genuine issue was much in question, as evidenced by its absence in Carter's book, *Why Not the Best?*, designed to boost his then lagging presidential campaign (Carter:Why). According to Patrick Anderson, Carter's chief speechwriter during the 1976 campaign, using human rights as an issue served both parties in that it involved "getting liberals out of jail in dictatorships" and appealed to conservatives because it involved criticism of Russia. He not only benefited from the fact that he introduced this ideology in the campaign, but that it was one of the few issues which did not divide the Democratic Party (Muravchik:4). Unlike other campaign issues, there was a meeting of the minds when it came to human rights. Daniel Moynihan recalled one conversation:

> "We'll be against the dictators you don't like the most," I said across the table to Sam Brown[1], "if you'll be against the dictators we don't like the most." The result was the strongest platform commitment to human rights in our history. Whether or not it was this commitment which directly influenced the new President to take the offensive, he began doing so from the very first, in his inaugural address. (Moynihan:22)

As expected, the next speech by Carter placed far more emphasis on human rights (U.S. Congress, House of Represenatives, Committee on House Administration:83-84). Whether this was by design or by accident, and it appears that it was more by accident, James Earl Carter had the vision to assimilate the human rights issue to draw support from all constituencies. One Carter campaigner said, "Human rights was an issue which you could bracket Kissinger and Ford on both sides...it was a beautiful campaign issue, an issue where there was a real degree of public hostility to the Ford Administration (Drew:37)."

It therefore seems apparent that President Carter utilized his political acumen in recognizing and seizing an opportunity to add substance to his campaign by establishing morality as one of the key components of his foreign policy. According to Zbigniew Brzezinski, Carter's National Security Advisor:

---

[1] Former anti-Vietnam War campaigner and representative of the Democratic party left.

The commitment to human rights reflected Carter's own religious beliefs, as well as his political acumen. He deeply believed in human rights and that commitment remained constant during his Administration. At the same time, he sensed, I think that the issue was an appealing one for it drew a sharp contrast between himself and the policies of Nixon and Kissinger. (Brzezinski:49)

Presidential Directive 13

President Jimmy E. Carter arrived in office having spent less than a dozen years in political service. Advertising his comparative lack of service as a virtue during his campaign in 1976, President Carter's rise to the top can be attributed to his persistent attacks on the lack of moral leadership in Washington and a public receptive to change after the Vietnam and Watergate debacles. One of his foremost presidential actions was implementing Presidential Directive 13, which placed demanding restrictions on security assistance and restricted sales to numerous foreign countries based on a number of issues, one of which was human rights practices.

While taking the oath of office, President Carter pledged, "Because we are free, we can never be indifferent to the fate of freedom elsewhere. Our moral sense dictates a clear-cut preference for those societies which share with us an abiding respect for individual human rights (Brown:9)." In support of Presidential Directive 13, the State Department prepared a paper which identified the need to further define human rights objectives, provided institutional resources to direct the policy, and answered a myriad of complex security assistance questions. Despite this monumental effort, there were many questions left unanswered concerning human rights objectives and how they would mesh with other national security objectives and interests. By June, the administration had at least broken the surface by publishing the Presidential Review Memorandum on human rights, a report which reflected the administration view on human rights and set forth implementation guidelines (Brown:9), although by almost all accounts the policy was ill-defined.

President Carter also believed the United States held a special responsibility to slow the number of arms provided. Following the lead of Congress which had already placed numerous restrictions on security assistance and economic aid through the AECA of 1976 and the Harkin Amendment, President Carter outlined selected parts of his plan in a speech given on May 19, 1977:

> The virtually unrestrained spread of conventional weaponry threatens stability in every region of the world. Total arms sales in recent years have risen to over $20 billion, and the United States accounts for more than one-half of this amount. Each year, the weapons transferred are not only more numerous, but also more sophisticated and deadly. Because of the threat to world peace embodied in this spiraling arms traffic; and because of the special responsibilities we bear as the largest single seller, I believe that the United States must take steps to restrain its arms transfers.
>
> Therefore, shortly after my Inauguration, I directed a comprehensive review of US conventional arms transfer policy, including all military, political, and economic factors. After reviewing the results of this study, and discussing those results with members of Congress and foreign leaders, I have concluded that the United States will henceforth view arms transfers as an exceptional foreign policy implement, to be used only in instances where it can be clearly demonstrated that the transfer contributes to our national security interests. We will continue to utilize arms transfers to promote our security and the security of our close friends. But, in the future, the burden of persuasion will be on those who favor a particular arms sale, rather than those who oppose it. (Report:1-3)

In implementing his policy on arms restraint, President Carter established a set of controls applicable to all transfers except countries with major defense treaties (NATO, Japan, Australia, and New Zealand). From his report on May 19th, he said "The controls will be binding unless extraordinary circumstances necessitate a Presidential exception, or where I determine that countries friendly to the United States must depend on advanced weaponry to offset quantitative and other disadvantages in order to maintain a regional balance (Report:1)." Carter's six point plan placed numerous restrictions on the flow of arms to other countries. From the report to Congress:

1. The dollar volume (in constant FY 1976 dollars) of commitments under the Foreign Military Sales and Military Assistance Program for weapons and weapons-related items in 1978 will be reduced from the FY 1977 total. Transfers which can clearly be classified as services are not covered, nor are commercial sales, which the U.S. Government monitors through the issuance of export licenses. Commercial sales are already significantly restrained by existing legislation and Executive Branch policy. Lucy W. Benson, Under Secretary of State for Security Assistance, Science and Technology in the Carter Administration, listed four desired effects (hopes) of the Carter directive on the volume of sales (Catrina:82):

- the requirement for analysis and long-range planning caused by the ceiling, forcing the administration to set clear priorities.

- the requirement to tighten up the bookkeeping.

- the inhibiting effect on questionable transfer proposals.

- evidence to other suppliers that the United States was serious about restraint.

In establishing a ceiling on the dollar volume of arms transfers, the Carter administration identified and listed several positives and negatives relating to this endeavor. In defense of the new policy on the dollar volume of arms transfers, the administration offered:

- Dollar volumes are among the surest means to limit U.S. arms transfers.

- Dollar ceilings, publicly announced, would send an unmistakable signal of this Administration's policy to domestic and foreign audiences.

- Dollar ceilings, if applied in lieu of a combination of more selective controls, could provide a simplified decision making process and, in some cases, allow greater Executive discretion.

- Dollar ceilings would encourage more explicit consideration of trade-offs and priorities among recipient's requests for arms. (Report:25)

On the negative side, the administration apparently understood that the policy was replete with potential adverse consequences. The disadvantages listed by the Carter Administration:

- Ceilings can be administered either on a first-come-first-served basis, or by explicitly assigning a share of the ceiling to each prospective recipient. Either approach presents serious management problems;

- If ceilings were administered on a first-come-first-served basis, recipients would tend to place orders very early in the year while there remained "room" within the ceiling. The United States Government, however, would have strong incentives to defer decisions until late in the year when competing demands (among which trade-offs would be necessary) were better known;

- If ceilings were administered on a quota basis, the U.S. Government would have to make explicit, and eventually public, distinctions among categories of recipients.

- If ceilings were administered on a quota basis, recipients would tend to utilize their full share of the ceiling each year to avoid risk of unmet demands in subsequent years, i.e., the arms transfer ceiling would become a floor;

- Regardless of the basis on which the ceiling was administered, decisions on individual cases would tend to be made with respect to their impact on the ceiling in addition to (or at worst, rather than) on the merits of the case. The following consequences would ensue:

  -- Recipients could become uncertain about the reliability of the U.S. as a supplier and resentful if their requests were rejected for reasons unrelated to the merits of the particular case;

  -- Less expensive systems would become more attractive, even when they were less suitable;

  -- Competition among U.S. firms and, perhaps, their respective promotional activities could become more intense as they worked to ensure that their interests were accommodated within the ceiling.

  -- Other suppliers are unlikely to join the U.S. in imposing a ceiling, at least in the short run. To the extent that they increased their sales to fill the buyers' residual demands that resulted from a U.S. ceiling, the effects of a U.S. ceiling on worldwide arms transfers would be attenuated;

-- Announcement of a ceiling, in combination with apprehensions that the ceiling could be lowered in subsequent years, might encourage buyers to place orders that otherwise would have been deferred. In brief, a ceiling could have the perverse effect of reversing the present forecast of declining arms sales over time;

-- A ceiling could increase the proportion of commercial licenses that resulted in exports, i.e., under some circumstances a ceiling could increase the volume of arms transfers, especially commercial sales. (Report:26)

2. The United States will not be the first supplier to introduce into a region newly-developed, advanced weapons systems which could create a new or significantly higher combat capability. Also, any commitment for sale or coproduction of such weapons is prohibited until they are operationally deployed with US forces, thus removing the incentive to promote foreign sales in an effort to lower unit costs for Defense Department procurement. According to the report to Congress by the Carter Administration (Report:31), there are four possible implications when advanced weapons are transferred:

- the compromise of advanced U.S. technology or classified data if the equipment falls into hostile hands;

- the development of countermeasures which might nullify the effectiveness of the equipment;

- a destabilizing augmentation in the requester's military capability;

- the heavy financial burden on the recipient in meeting unforeseen acquisition or support costs.

3. Development or significant modification of advanced weapons systems solely for export will not be permitted. The reasoning behind this prohibition is that it places U.S. companies at far greater risks and makes it difficult to maintain costs on non U.S.-standardized components (Report:32).

4. Coproduction agreements[2] for significant weapons, equipment, and major components (beyond assembly of subcomponent and the fabrication of high-turnover spare parts) are prohibited. A limited class of items will be considered for coproduction agreements, since these arrangements are intended primarily for the coproducer's requirements. From 1957-1976, 65 major coproduction projects were approved, with about half of the approvals for NATO countries (Report:35).

5. In addition to existing requirements of the law, the United States, as a condition of sale for certain weapons, equipment, or major components, may stipulate that it will not entertain any requests for retransfers. By establishing this guideline, the United States can avoid unnecessary bilateral friction's caused by later denials. The success of this program depends on the goodwill of the recipient, the desire of recipient to maintain good relations with the U.S., and the desire of the recipient to retain the United States as a source of military supply (Report:36).

6. An amendment to the International Traffic in Arms regulations will be issued, requiring policy level authorizations by the Department of State for actions by agents of the United States or private manufacturers, which might promote the sale of arms abroad. In addition, embassies and military representatives abroad will not promote the sale of arms and the Secretary of Defense will continue his review of government procedures, particularly procurement regulations, which may provide incentives for foreign sales (Report:37).

President Carter added, "in formulating security assistance programs consistent with these controls, we will continue our efforts to promote and advance respect for human rights in recipient countries." He also emphasized the success of these initiatives

---

[2] Coproduction covers a range of transfers of design, development and production techniques both through government and commercial channels and includes various combinations of the assembly and manufacture of components and entire weapon systems.

was dependent on multilateral cooperation and that the United States as the number one arms supplier in the world was responsible for taking the first step (Report:3).

As figure 4-1 below indicates, sales of U.S. arms around the globe peaked in 1975, but showed a noticeable decline during the first years of Carter's presidency.

U.S. Arms the Globe
($ Billions)

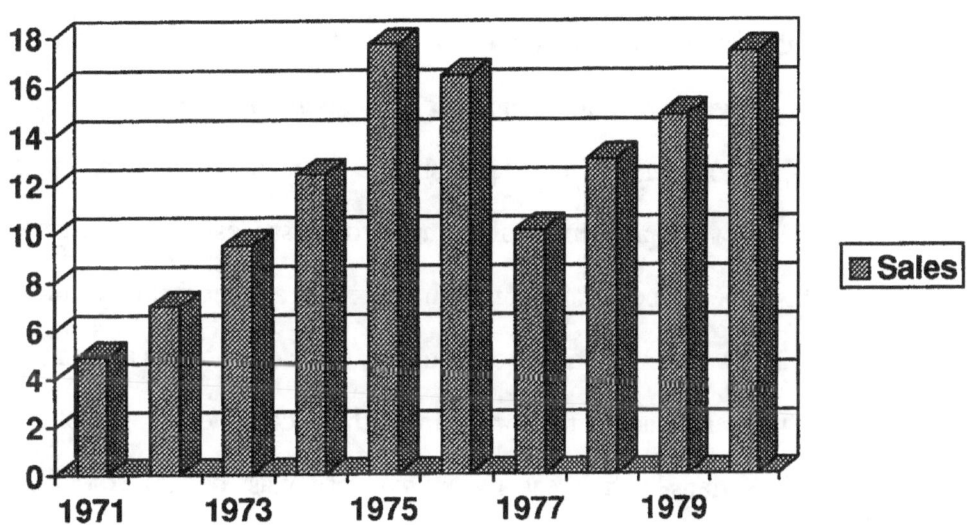

Figure 4-1. United States Arms Sales

Sales rose steadily after 1978 as the Carter Administration gradually lost their resolve to entertain the policy alone. Countries friendly to the United States never joined the U.S. effort and the policy lost what little leverage it started with. Even at the policy's inception, the Carter policy still allowed for a plethora of extraordinary circumstances in which the President could determine a country friendly to the United States needed advanced weaponry to maintain a regional balance (Hutchins:10).

The Carter directive was met with harsh criticism from many countries, a justifiable reaction given the nature of a supplier's refusal to sell. According to Lawrence Freedman in his book *Britain and the Arms Trade* (Freedman:389-90):

> Though only limited political benefits can normally be expected from agreeing to sell arms, since this is seen in commercial terms, *refusing to sell* arms is a major political act. It appears as a calculated insult, reflecting on the stability, trust, and credit-worthiness, or technical competence of the would-be recipient.

It appears the Carter Administration understood the implications behind limiting arms sales to countries violating human rights as they produced a Presidential Memorandum to specifically define the relationship between human rights and political systems. There were several problems which impacted the success of the Carter approach to the human rights issue, namely other conflicting interests and the failure of the administration to narrow down an effective definition which could serve as a universal model for all countries. Because of this, problems with the consistency of implementation frequently arose. Historians list five reasons that make inconsistency unavoidable:

(1) We should have different expectations of different countries which take into account the unique history of each.

(2) The U.S. has different amounts of leverage with different countries.

(3) Evaluations of human rights performance of various governments will differ in accordance with different opinions about which human rights deserve priority.

(4) Various external and internal conditions, notably war or insurrection, may affect what it is reasonable to expect in the realm of human rights.

(5) Other interests of the United States may impede its ability to act on its principles with regard to specific countries. (Muravchik:118):

Carter Administration Arms Transfer Objectives

<u>The Purpose of Arms Transfers</u>. Arms transfers have long been a major instrument of U.S. foreign policy. The purposes behind approving sales are as follows (Report:17-18):

- to support diplomatic efforts to resolve major regional conflicts by maintaining local balances and enhancing our access and influence vis-à-vis the parties;

- to influence the political orientation of nations which control strategic resources;

- to help maintain regional balances among nations important to us in order to avert war or political shifts away from us;

- to enhance the quality and commonality of the capability of major Allies participating with us in joint defense arrangements;

- to promote self-sufficiency in deterrence and defense as a stabilizing factor in itself and as a means of reducing the level and automaticity of possible American involvement;

- to strengthen the internal security and stability of recipients;

- to limit Soviet influence and maintain the balance in conventional arms;

- to enhance our general access to and influence with governments and military elite's whose political orientation counts for us on global or regional issues;

- to provide leverage and influence with individual governments on specific issues of immediate concern to us;

- to secure base rights, overseas facilities, and transit rights to support the deployment and operations of our forces and intelligence systems.

According to the report, U.S. arms transfers have served a number of purposes, including: strengthening friends and allies to defend themselves; enhancing our influence with recipients, while cementing positive relations; and have denied hostile powers the opportunity to gain positions of influence in a number of Third World countries.

Arms Transfer Guidelines. Arms transfers do not come without costs, though, as the arming of countries involves entailed commitments, occasional U.S. presence, and does not include guarantees that a given set of objectives will remain stable over time, one of the many reasons behind President Carter's arms restraint plea. In support of his plan, the following guidelines have been published concerning restraint in U.S. arms transfers (Report:18-19):

- to encourage a general reduction in both world arms transfers and reliance on military might as an essential element in a more peaceful and stable world order;

- through a lower level of armament, to curtail the potential for arms races and limit the intensity of conflict if it occurs;

- to reduce the potential and pressure for U.S. involvement in local conflicts to the extent this follows from various arms supply relationships;

- to moderate super power competition and the prospect for conflict in regional situations (if multilateral initiatives are successful);

- to reduce reliance on arms transfers as a means of implementing our diplomacy, to the detriment of alternative non-military instruments;

- to protect U.S. military capabilities by limiting the dispersion of military technology that could be used against us and our Allies;

- to distance ourselves from regimes that do not respect and observe basic human rights and fundamental freedoms;

- to limit the diversion of moneys and skills in developing nations away from fundamental economic development needs;

- to permit U.S. resources to be shifted from financing weapons to terrorists;
- to build U.S. domestic support for our foreign policy objectives in the developing world.

Key Assumptions. While establishing the many assumptions behind its arms restraint policy, the Carter administration also provided key assumptions which would be followed to facilitate objective attainment. The assumptions from the *Report to Congress on Arms Transfer Policy* (Report:20) are:

- The U.S., within the context of a policy of restraint, will continue to utilize arms transfers where necessary to promote our own strategic interests, the security of our allies and close friends, and world peace.

- In particular, the U.S. will maintain its close defense relationships, with NATO members, Japan, Australia, and New Zealand.

- The U.S. has special responsibilities to insure Israel's security in order to deter war and to make progress toward peace.

- The U.S. will pursue multilateral initiatives with other suppliers in an effort to restrain the international trade in armaments.

- Primary attention will be focused on new requests for the transfer of weapons, particularly systems of advanced technology. The U.S. will not normally be related services.

- The U.S. will not cancel existing contracts. Goods and services will continue to be offered in support of the systems previously furnished, though management arrangements may be changed and the U.S. will reserve the right to determine appropriate quantities and timing.

Resolution Means. The report addressed problems with soliciting and obtaining the multilateral support from other prolific arms-producing countries, notably the countries of France, Great Britain, Israel, Germany, Italy, Belgium, Sweden, and the Soviet Union. The report also mentioned the likely scenario of the Soviets increasing their productive capacity to expand their influence in the absence of the U.S. To address the importance of multilateral restraint, the Carter administration suggested five means by which issues and situations could be addressed and resolved (Report:22):

(1) Bilateral consultations with suppliers and recipients, at U.S. initiative.

(2) A <u>suppliers' conference</u>, involving the small number of major suppliers. This would have to be accompanied by a series of bilaterals, particularly with the Soviet Union, as well as some means for working with recipients.

(3) <u>International organization conferences</u>, including both suppliers and recipients.

(4) <u>Supplier-buyer conferences</u> developed on a regional basis. This type of arrangement would focus the interpretation of general guidelines on the particular security needs and instabilities of a specific region.

(5) <u>Recipient conferences</u>. The development of multilateral approaches to this problem will be a long and complex process, to which there has been a great resistance in the past. Although the shift in U.S. policy unilaterally will provide some momentum, particularly with other suppliers, the longer process will require the identification and implementation of restraints that serve the interests of both suppliers and recipients.

<u>Arms Transfer Considerations</u>. In addition to the multitude of factors already addressed, the Carter administration established considerations to be examined when determining whether to approve an arms sale request. The lengthy list includes:

- The role that proposed recipients play in their regions, what interests they share with the United States, and where our interests diverge.

- Whether the transactions will do more to further U.S. objectives on balance than other economic or political measures.

- The nature of U.S. influence that sales might help support, including the potential restraint that can be applied in conflict situations.

- Whether a particular sale would set a precedent for further requests for arms, or similar requests from other countries.

- The current internal stability of the recipient country, its capacity to maintain that stability, and its attitude toward human rights.

- The possible adverse impact of not selling on our relations with a friendly government.

- The options available to the recipient country. (Will that country turn to other suppliers? What sources? What will be the political, military, and economic implications of this? If a country has options that it will unhesitatingly employ, would our refusal to sell mean the forfeiting of opportunities to develop or maintain parallel interests and objectives?).

- Whether the proposed sale is consistent with the recipient country's development goals or our economic assistance program, if there is one.

- Whether the sale might strain the country's ability to manage its debt obligations or entail operations and maintenance costs that might make successive claims on future budgets.

- The economic benefits to the United States from the sale or coproduction of arms, especially to the oil rich states.

- The threat the military capability represented by a transfer is supposed to counter or deter, whether we agree on the nature of the threat, and how it relates to our own security.

- How the proposed transfer affects the regional military balance, regional military tensions, or the military build-up plans of another country.

- Whether the recipient country has the capability to absorb and utilize the arms effectively.

- What other military interests, such as U.S. overflight rights or access to facilities would be supported by the transaction.

- The impact of the transfer on our own readiness.

- Whether a substantial physical dependence on U.S. sources of supply would result which could enhance our influence (e.g., for conflict prevention or resolution), or which conversely could embroil us in crises involuntarily. (Report:134-135)

To facilitate an understanding of the US goals regarding arms transfers, the Carter administration traveled to Europe to discuss mutual cooperation in arms reduction. These talks, commonly known as the Conventional Arms Transfer Talks (CAT), attempted to solicit cooperation and where cooperation did not exist, attempted to convey the importance of **not** taking advantage of the US policy concerning restraint of arms. However, the European countries were not enthusiastic about this proposed arrangement, stating that any agreement would depend on Soviet actions. US and Soviet officials met four times between July 1977 and December 1978 but negotiations stalemated when the Soviets balked at the U.S. position and linked negotiations to a plethora of what many considered peripheral issues (Hutchins:11). Talks broke off and US-Soviet relations worsened

Goals of Carter Security Assistance Program

Having germinated as a policy rather late in the Carter campaign, the human rights issue started as something less than an exact policy. In the book the *Uncertain Crusade*, Joshua Muravchik quotes four rather broad, announced goals of the Carter human rights policy (Muravchik:17):

(1) To enhance respect for the U.S. worldwide.

(2) To help sustain domestic support for our policies by rooting them in our moral values.

(3) To strengthen our position in the international arena.

(4) To strengthen our influence among some of the developing nations.

What did Carter expect from the United States to facilitate accomplishment of his administration's goals? At a town meeting in Clinton, Massachusetts, in March 1977, he said, rather naively:

"I want to see our country set a standard of morality. I feel very deeply that when people are put in prison without trial and tortured and deprived of basic human rights that the President of the United States ought to have a right to express displeasure and do something about it. . . . I want our country to be the focal point for deep concern about human beings all over the world." (Brzezinski:125).

It was not until February 17, 1978, with the signing of Presidential Directive 30 that the policy achieved better clarity. Its essential points were:

(1) Priorities were set among U.S. human-rights objectives--reducing worldwide governmental violations of the integrity of the person, and enhancing civil and political liberties. It was also a continuing objective to promote basic economic and social rights.

(2) There would be greater reliance on positive incentives that acknowledge improvements.

(3) No U.S. support, "other than in exceptional circumstances," would be allowed for policing functions by governments guilty of serious violations of human rights.

(4) U.S. human-rights initiatives in international financial institutions would be geared "so as not to undermine the essential U.S. interest of preserving these institutions as effective economic interests." (Brzezinski:126)

To facilitate the U.S. security assistance program guidelines, certain directive leverage instruments were utilized to influence human rights in recipient countries. Leverage consisted of arms transfers, and economic aid in the case of countries unfriendly to the United States, but still receiving aid. The governing legislation for this aid was Public Law 480 (Muravchik:121), and in FY1980, Carter's last year, eighty countries received aid under PL480, but only six required special language regarding needy people. The six were Guinea, Haiti, Indonesia, Liberia, Somalia, and Zaire (Muravchik:122). Noteworthy because of their absence from the list were countries who were accused of human rights violations. This list included Syria, China, Angola, Ethiopia, Nicaragua, Panama, Kampuchea, Benin, the People's Republic of the Congo, Guinea-Bissau, Mali, and Tanzania (Muravchik:122).

Implementation Process

Policy . The bureaucratic makeup of the human rights dimension was extensive. Prior to the Carter Administration, a Bureau for Human Rights and Humanitarian Affairs had been established in the State Department[3]. This agency had little impact due to the lack of commitment by the Nixon-Ford regimes. The successor in charge of the Bureau for Human Rights, Patricia Derian, displayed an enthusiastic commitment for the crusade and had direct access to Carter (Dumbrell:180). Her department communicated frequently with permantly assigned human rights officers within the State Department. In addition, a special interagency group, known as the Christopher Group, was in charge of factoring human rights issues with aid and lending decisions (Dumbrell:180), and an officer from the National Security Council staff also played a pivotal role. Each of the aforementioned agencies participated in the decision process and conflicts arose between the State Department and Secretary of State Vance and his deputy, Warren Christopher. Derian and her co-workers were often accused of trying to 'out-Carter' President Carter in the human rights area. D. C. McGaffey, a Foreign Service Officer, offers a different opinion:

> No one in the Foreign Service assumed that President Carter was politically naive, or totally cynical. Unfortunately, the human rights policy as enunciated did not give sufficient guidance or definition to determine exactly where between these extremes the real, desired policy would fall. (McGaffey:69)

Issues which impacted the success and effectiveness of the Human Rights Bureaus were plentiful. One issue which was vetoed by Warren Christopher was a proposal to have every State Department agency produce a plan to promote human rights within each country (Maynard:197). Another issue, an ongoing concern, was the degree by which State Department agencies controlled information to influence the decision-making process (Dumbrell:181). Stephen Cohen, Deputy to Derian between 1978 and 1980 echoed this point by saying, "The extent of abusive practices was consistently

---

[3] Staffing in this bureau increased from two during the Ford Administration to twenty-nine by 1979.

underreported (Dumbrell:182)." Cohen also said that the way to prevent negative actions against a proposed country was to overstate the U.S. security interest at stake.

Other governmental agencies also conflicted with the Human Rights Bureau. The Treasury Department opposed attempts to link U.S. economic assistance to human rights, the Pentagon had no overt policy regarding human rights, and the Department of Commerce had numerous run-ins with Derian over the sale of crime-control equipment to repressive regimes (Maynard:53). Perhaps one of most heated relationships existed between National Security Advisor Brzezinski and Derian over Brzezinski's overriding of many State Department proposals to restrict or eliminate aid for countries accused of violating human rights.

The normal method of ironing out differences within the human rights area was during a monthly meeting attended by, on average, 40 people. At this meeting security assistance and national interest issues were reviewed and the Derian Group then sent recommendations to Christopher, who adjucated them. The criteria used by the Christopher Group to arrive at decisions was formidable;

> (1) 'Integrity of the person' violations would receive high priority.
>
> (2) Human rights practices can be expected to differ from country to country.
>
> (3) Other fundamental U.S. interests must be considered alongside human rights.
>
> (4) Policy must be influenced by the leverage available to the U.S. in particular cases.
>
> (5) Policy must be responsive even to incremental changes in the level of human rights violations.
>
> (6) 'Quiet diplomacy' was often more effective than formal sanctions.
> (Mower:75)

Looking at the specifics behind determining whether specific countries violated the Carter Administration human rights policy:

> For each country a bureau member in the Department of State lays out the human rights-related problems. Violations are listed and positive developments in the human rights area are outlined. The particular loan under consideration is briefly described. It is then decided whether to instruct the U.S. director to the (international financial institution) to vote yes, no, or to abstain on the particular project. It seems that normally the (regional) bureau people are more in favor of granting the loans, or at least abstaining while Warren Christopher and others at the secretary and assistant secretary level and those in the human rights bureau will be less lenient. (Dumbrell:183)

Who possessed the real power behind implementing the human rights policy? According to Derian, it was 'one man, one vote--Christopher was the man and his was the vote (Dumbrell:184). However, one member of the National Security Council staff suggests that a consensus was put forth by all involved with the human rights policies. He described the consensus as:

> After Jimmy Carter's 1977 decision to restrict the sale of military hardware on a worldwide basis, virtually the entire security assistance community within the government set about undermining the policy until it was effectively rescinded three years later. (Shoemaker:30)

The constant struggle between agencies with conflicting interests could explain the inconsistencies which abounded around the human rights policies.

Strategy. How did the Carter team launch the human rights policy? Only a week after the inauguration, the State Department read a statement criticizing Czechoslovakia for its arresting and handling of Czech dissidents who called for Czech observance of the Helsinki accords, which had a strong human rights provision (Facts:103); criticized Rhodesia for its negotiations stance over the future of that country;

and sent a letter to, and issued a statement on behalf, of Soviet Union dissident Andrey

Sakharov:

> We have long admired Andrey Sakharov as an outspoken champion of human
> rights in the Soviet Union. He is, as you know, a prominent, respected scientist, a
> Nobel laureate, who, at considerable risk, has worked to promote respect for
> human rights in his native land.
>
> Any attempts by the Soviet authorities to intimidate Mr. Sakharov will not silence
> legitimate criticism in the Soviet Union and will conflict with accepted
> international standards in the field of human rights. (Vance, January 31, 1977 news
> conference:138)

The Soviet reaction to the much anticipated criticism by the United States was

undoubtedly pre-orchestrated and intended to test the U.S. mettle over human rights.

Soviet Ambassador Dobrynin called U.S. Secretary Vance to protest (Facts:105) and

followed this up with a letter from the Soviet press agency Tass, denouncing the US's

words about Sakharov as an "unsavory ploy" (Facts:105). The response around the

United State was mixed. The Seattle Times wrote the following positive review:

> There is no longer any doubt about what the administration thinks of Soviet
> repression or about the administration's willingness to speak up about the subject.
> President Carter's unprecedented letter to Andrei Sakharov, hero of the dissident
> movement in Moscow, has banished in spectacular fashion all thoughts that the
> administration would try to ignore the rising chorus of dissidence behind the Iron
> Curtain.
>
> The administration is not going to play a game of "hear no evil, see no evil, speak
> no evil" with the Kremlin in the hope that the Soviets will thereby be more
> favorably disposed toward concluding a new nuclear-arms limitation pact and any
> other accords with this country. In our view, the forthright course is the proper
> course. (Facts:126)

Offering an opposing viewpoint, The St. Louis Globe wrote:

However, well-intentioned he may be, President Jimmy Carter is playing a doubtful
game by becoming a pen pal of Soviet dissident Andrei Sakharov. It may be

letter Sakharov had written to him on Jan 21, asking the new American President for support of the civil rights movement in Russia.

One wonders how President Carter would react if an American dissident received a letter from Chairman Leonid Brezhnev, urging adoption of a constitutional amendment outlawing abortion, and offering his concern as evidence that Soviet Russia was committed to protection of human rights.

If President Carter's extraordinary act results in tightening of Soviet repression, rather than relaxation, he may have cause to regret what he did. While no President of the United States should be intimidated from expressing himself freely, neither should he maneuver himself into a situation where he can be accused of meddling in the internal affairs of another state -- to the peril of those he seeks to befriend. (Facts:131)

In response to these criticisms, President Carter issued a statement saying that while the statement correctly reflected his beliefs, he did not want to engage in activity which would damage U.S.-Soviet relations (Facts:158). In addition to these announcements over human rights, the administration asked a Chilean government official to leave the country after learning of the torture of prisoners in Chile (Facts:178). As a result of the criticism by the U.S., the Soviet Union arrested a noted dissident Alexandr Ginzburg and expelled Associated Press correspondent George Krimsky due to his contacts with the dissidents (Facts:106). Carter's response to this was to expel a Soviet correspondent (Facts:106). The initial result of the new U.S. policy was stepped up suppression of human rights activists by the Soviet Union (Brzezinski:156).

Problems arose in other countries as well. In Uganda, the Anglican Archbishop and two cabinet ministers were presumably murdered by Uganda leader Ida Amin, amidst a bloody campaign against Uganda's Christians. The U.S. State Department responded by deploring the "massive violations of human rights in Uganda" and the "violent death" of the three men (Vance interview:250). President Carter added to the barrage of criticism by saying "the events in Uganda have disgusted the entire civilized world" (Facts:189). Uganda dictator Amin retaliated to the U.S. lambasting by ordering the 200 Americans living in Uganda to come to Kampala to meet with him and decreeing that none of them

could leave without his approval (Facts:247). After several days of tense negotiating and

the positioning of a U.S. naval task force off the African coast, the Americans were

allowed to depart. Not surprisingly, the handling of this incident by President Carter

evoked strong emotion across the United States, both for and against his handling of the

incident. Along positive lines, the Wisconsin State Journal wrote:

> President Carter is reacting cautiously, responsibly and in the best interests of
> American citizens in Uganda in his diplomatic chess game with the brutish
> Ugandan dictator, Idi Amin.
>
> Carter spoke out strongly against Amin's terrorism after a killing spree that
> followed what appears to be the wanton murder of an Anglican archbishop and
> two cabinet ministers, who Amin contends were attempting to overthrow the
> regime.
>
> When the erratic Amin announced a call-up of all Americans in Uganda for a
> "meeting" Wednesday, Carter wisely lowered his voice, although serving notice
> that the United States would do whatever is necessary to save American lives. In
> the language of diplomacy, "whatever is necessary" means the possibility of using
> military force.
>
> Meantime, it is the obligation of the United States and the rest of the world to
> speak out forcefully on behalf of human rights, as Carter has been doing, and to
> apply diplomatic and economic pressure to assure protection of those rights in
> Uganda. (Facts:249)

In response to congressional questioning of President Carter's new policy,

Secretary of State Vance appeared before the Senate Subcommittee on Foreign

Operations Appropriations to champion the President's policy and also announce the

planned reduction of aid to Argentina, Uruguay, and Ethiopia because of human rights

violations (U.S. Congress, House of Representatives,Committee on Appropriations:149-

205). At the same time this announcement was made, the administration stated it had to

balance a political concern for human rights against economic or security goals, citing

South Korea as one example where it was unwise to cut security assistance, even in the face of extensive human rights violations (U.S. Congress, House of Representatives, Committee on Appropriations:186). As a result of the proposed reduction in aid to their countries, Argentina and Uruguay announced a rejection of any future aid from the U.S. The countries of Brazil, Guatemala, and El Salvador did likewise after hearing of condemnations from the U.S. government shortly thereafter (U.S. Congress, House of Representatives, Committee on Appropriations:760).

The U.S. position on Soviet treatment with regard to human rights[4] continued to walk a fine line, although President Carter did receive noted Soviet dissident Vladimir Bukovsky, exiled to the United States during the Ford Administration. This political event received strong protests from the Soviet Government and from across the U.S. The Arkansas Gazette wrote:

> President Carter, properly, has honored his White House invitation to Vladimir Bukovsky, though we shall continue to think that it was ill-advised, if only for the relative haste with which it was issued and its timing to coincide with disclosure of his famous letter to a second Soviet dissident, Andrei Sakharov.
>
> In the period between the disclosure of the Sakharov Letter and the appearance of Bukovsky at the White House the President had sought to convince the Soviet leaders that he had never intended to convey the impression that the Russians were the *only* suppressers of human liberties in the world. We have already noted how these things tend to build on one another, so the President, upon meeting with Bukovsky, naturally felt compelled to say that his expressed commitment to human rights was permanent, and that "I don't intend to be timid in my public statements and positions."
>
> This is all very well so long as Mr. Carter is equally determined not to allow the rhetoric of commitment to a lasting ideal to fuzz the finite limitations on one nation's powers to coerce another in the conduct of its internal affairs. There is another thing that Mr. Carter should keep further in mind is that even more rhetoric, uttered as much as anything for its own effect, still can be further debased by over-use--the so-called broken record effect. (Facts:141)

---

[4] I've chosen to include examples of human rights treatment within the Soviet Union, even though the United States holds no leverage over that country based on arms transfers, which there are none. Their inclusion merely serves the purpose of showcasing President Carter's response to global criticism.

This set off a string of oppressive actions within the Soviet Union (Vance, March 28, 1977 news conference:247). On Mar 4, the Soviets accused some leading Jewish dissidents of working for the CIA (Cooper:26); on Mar 13, Soviet Pravda accused the Carter human rights policies of "bringing about an air of distrust (Cooper:27); on March 15, Soviet authorities arrested Anatoly Shcharansky, the most prominent Jewish dissident (Cooper:27); and on March 21, Soviet leader Brezhnev stated:

> Washington's claims to teach others how to live, I believe, cannot be accepted by any sovereign state. . . .we will not tolerate interference in our internal affairs by anyone and under any pretext. A normal development of relations on such a basis is, of course, unthinkable. (Whelan:4)

What is even more surprising, given the strained relations which have permeated U.S.-Soviet relations since the end of WWII, was Carter's unusual reaction. Arthur Schlesinger, Jr. Wrote:

> The Soviet resentment, for some utterly mysterious reason, astonished Carter himself; he spoke in June 1977 of the "surprising adverse reaction in the Soviet Union to our stand on human rights." But he accepted it as a fact of life and moderated his campaign accordingly. (Schlesinger:516-517)

President Carter responded to the beration of his human rights policies by stating the U.S. would continue to protest Soviet misbehavior of the Helsinki Accords, but would not discontinue talks on other issues based on Soviet noncompliance.

Human Rights - Consistently Applied or Not?

One of the more serious problems faced by the Carter Administration was in defining the policy regarding human rights so that ambiguity in its application was minimized. By clearly defining the human rights policy, uncertainty would be reduced and countries turned down for aid would have a sense that they were treated on an equal basis.

As indicated by the following examples, the Carter Administration had enormous difficulty in defining what constituted violations worthy of eliminating or reducing arms sales.

South Korea. U.S. aid was not reduced, despite great concern about the human rights situation in South Korea. Secretary of State Vance cited the overriding security commitment to the strategically placed ally.

Historically, South Korea is closely linked with the United States in several areas:

(1) South Korea is the linchpin of the United States strategic defense posture in Asia.

(2) The United States has a commitment to attaining a democratic South Korea.

(3) South Korea is the ninth largest trading partner with the United States. (Mower:138)

Despite this close association, South Korea continued its repression of human rights during the 1977-1980 period and refused to yield to the pressures put forth by the Carter Administration to improve. Although the administration did use hard rhetoric in an attempt to persuade the South Korean government to change its stance toward human rights issues, the Carter Administration is the one that back-pedaled numerous times. Although the administration did, on several occasions, vote against comparably small loans to South Korea, for what appears to be more of a face-saving gesture for the administration, the $130 to $276 million in aid distributed annually tells the story (Dumbrell:186). The administration also threatened to withdraw U.S. troops from S. Korea by 1979 but eventually withdrew this threat as well.

The United States holds a special responsibility toward South Korea based on its key role in liberating Korea from Japan at the end of WWII and the subsequent involvement in the Korea War. A quote directly from the U.S. Defense Department's "Congressional Presentation" for the fiscal year 1978 security assistance program, explains the Carter Administration position: "Human rights practices in Korea have been carefully considered in formulating this proposed security assistance program (Brown:260)." The report was referring to the $280,000,000 in aid appropriated for the ROK. This is despite proof that the Korean government regularly practices of torture and political murder, manipulation of the judicial system for purposes of political repression, and restraint on freedoms of expression (Brown:260).

In one extreme example of the violation of freedom of expression, Kim Chi-Ha, a poet laureate of the democratic resistance, states the government neglects the rights of the poor and underprivileged and uses torture to extract false confessions (Brown:267). When he exposed this governmental technique, not only did he receive a life sentence, but he was denied the use of toilet paper because he was once caught writing a statement against the Korean government using that medium (Brown:267). Justification for such actions by the Korean government can be explained by the following South Korean legislation[5], referred to as Emergency Decree No. 9, which explains the government's position on vocalizing discontent:

> Emergency Decree No. 9 prohibits "fabricating or disseminating false rumors or misrepresenting facts and denying, opposing, misrepresenting or defaming the constitution; or asserting, petitioning, instigating or propagandizing revision or repeal of the constitution by means of assembly, demonstration or through public media such as newspapers, broadcasts or press services; or by other such means of expression such as writings, books or recordings. Also prohibited is any act openly defaming the emergency decree itself. Alleged violators are subject to arrest, detention, confiscation, and search without a judicially approved warrant. Those convicted are to receive not less than one year in prison, and no maximum sentence is specified. They are also subject to suspension of civil rights, including the rights to run for office and to vote, for up to ten years. (Brown:266)

Iran. The State Department urged that there be no change in U.S. policy toward Iran, a policy, despite widespread reports of human rights abuses, including a reported 2,800-3,000 imprisoned Iranians referred to as political prisoners (Facts:175). The annual

---

[5] Enacted on May 13, 1975.

country report said there was no verifiable evidence of torture, but no one would go as far as discounting the reports.

Because of its proximity to the Soviet Union, the country of Iran has always been given strategic priority within U.S. interests[6]. In conjunction with maintaining close relations with Iran for strategic interests, the United States has continually attempted to secure freedom for the Iranian people. This is also true during the Carter Presidency. The reign of the Shah of Iran, although stable by most accounts, was based on a combination of coercion and utilitarian satisfaction (Brown:290). The Shah faced innumerable difficulties in deciding whether to grant further freedom of expression as to do so would invited criticism of waste, corruption, extravagance, and unfair income distribution (Brown:290). From a long-standing U.S. standpoint, denying the sale of arms to Iran because of human rights issues, would be weakening our struggle against the Soviet Union--the view was that it was easier to condone human rights violations than it was to lose a strategic interest, although by most accounts the country of Iran possessed sufficient strength to defend itself against an initial Soviet aggression.

The situation in Iran at the time of the Carter pronouncements about human rights was an ongoing concern. In the past, a pronouncement by the U.S. often led to the changing of leadership within Iran, thus his rhetoric was misconstrued by many as meaning the American government was ready to assist another overthrow. In response to the Carter policy, the Shah reacted responsively, at least initially. He released some political prisoners, improved prison conditions, and ceased torturing others (Brown:294). He also formed a human rights commission and allowed Red Cross officials to inspect selected prisons. On the negative side, it was feared that a serious situation was turning more volatile in that repression seemed to be intensifying at the same time that the Iranian people started to respond to the Carter pleas. The people started demanding free

---

[6] More priority given after WWII with the beginning of the Cold War.

elections, a free press, and the release of all political prisoners (Brown:295). One of the most prominent political priests, Ayatollah Khomeini, spoke out most harshly against the Shah. He spoke of the evil of the American government and viewed U.S. arms sales to Iran as a payoff to the Shah. Most Iranians viewed the sale of arms from the U.S. to Iran as more of a benefit to Americans than anything else (Brown:295). The overall view of the Carter policy was that it created a situation for confrontation in Iran.

The beginning of the end for the Shah may have been signaled by a riot which broke out in Tabriz (Northwest Iran). The significance was not so much that a riot took place, but that it was so well organized. When local police attempted to break up the gathering, the crowd became enraged and proceeded to destroy a number of banks, cinemas, and hotels (Brown:296). When the army was brought in to restore order, the pace and efficiently of the operation made many think that the Shah's internal security was vulnerable. Other riots broke out across Iran as a result of the Tabriz incident. One burning of a theater in Abadan killed between 400 and 700 customers (Brown;297). This incident was blamed on both the Shah's opponents and the Shah itself, ultimately hurting the Shah more.

The situation in Iran deteriorated even further. In September of 1978, more than 3 million Iranians participated in a demonstration against the Shah's regime. Although the demonstration was orderly, three days later martial law was imposed and troops fired on a large number of protesters. Estimates of the number of fatalities ranged from 78, the government figure, to 4,500, the total accepted by the opposition (Brown:297).

While many can and will argue that the Shah himself caused his undoing, others blame the Carter human rights policy for triggering the chain of events which ultimately caused the demise of the Shah.

Africa. Human rights within Africa are more a black/white issue than anything else. Because of this, the United States has constantly struggled with maintaining Africa as an ally while opposing its apartheid policies. In black Africa, the administration also created questions concerning the consistency in which it applied its human rights policy. Joseph Mobutu, ruler of Zaire, received annual aid in amounts exceeding $10 million, despite widespread reports concerning his regimes abuse of human rights (Dumbrell:186). In defense of the Carter policy of extending aid, the administration viewed Zaire as an important interest based on the amount of cobalt supplied on behalf of the American aircraft industry. Similar to other human rights issues, the emphasis on human rights in Africa was viewed much sterner during the first half of the Carter tenure, than his last two years.

Indonesia. Cited for strategic importance, the country of Indonesia, despite reports that Indonesian forces were facilitating a genocidal war against the people of East Timor, continued to receive U.S. aid. The American-supplied A-4 bomber played a large part in the Indonesian campaign, but Indonesia regularly denied that it was preventing East Timor's right to self-determination. A reported 31,000-50,000 Indonesians were being held by the government as a result of the abortive Communist Coup in 1965 (Facts:175). It is also documented that approximately 10,000 East Timor natives had been killed by the Indonesian government (Dumbrell:187). However, the aid continued under the auspices of the importance of maintaining positive relations with Indonesia (Brown:179).

Philippines. From September 22, 1972 through the Carter term as President, Filipinos had no free press, no free election for representatives, no union organizing, and an inflation rate over 50 percent (Brown:230). Torture reportedly was a regular activity and an estimated 53,000 people were arrested for political reasons. Although these numbers are alarming, the dispensing of security assistance to the Philippines is a complex issue. Robert B. Oakley, Deputy Assistant Secretary of State for East Asian and Pacific Affairs, while appearing before the Subcommittee on Foreign Operations of the House Appropriations Committee on April 5, 1977, said:

We have major military bases in the Philippines, the maintenance of which is important both for the defense of the Philippines from external attack and for the broader security interests of the United States Government. U.S. security assistance has long been viewed by the Philippine Government as an implicit quid pro quo for our use of these facilities. (Brown:237)

What Mr. Oakley was referring to was the leverage held by the Philippine Government over the U.S. due to the twenty American military installations, including major installations at Clark Air Field and Subic Naval Base. As a reward for the use of these installations the United States regularly paid the Philippine Government rent, either in the form of military aid or economic aid. The amount of aid is so substantial, and the leverage possessed by the Philippines so strong, that once President Marcos turned down an offer of $1 billion dollars in aid over a five year period, saying it was not enough (Brown:238). Despite the amount of aid provided by the United States, an editorial by Teodoro Valencia in the Philippines Daily Express (February 17, 1977) echoed the sentiments of many citizens of the Philippines:

> Filipinos, including some Church leaders, had hoped to use U.S. President Carter's announced abhorrence of violators of civil rights and human rights to needle President Marcos. Even the latest pastoral letter carried rings of warning that the President of the USA may look with disfavor on some of the practices of martial law. But these colonial-minded Filipinos must have suffered a shock when President Carter called down the U.S. State Department for denouncing Russia's imprisonment of writer Andrei Sakharov. . . . Obviously, America is to have a double standard, one for big guys like Russia and China and another for small ones like the Philippines, Indonesia, and Singapore. (Valencia:4)

A Philippine opposition senator[7] offered even deeper insight into the situation plaguing the Carter Administration and its intent on advancing human rights:

---

[7] Name withheld

While America is our best friend, you cannot string us along with moral promises and then expect equanimity when you fail us. Indeed, the level of cynicism over U.S. human rights posturing is so deep that if I were running for office today, I could only get elected from my constituency by adopting an anti-American position. (Brown:246)

The end result of the U.S. use of arms sales as a tool of foreign policy in the Philippines and a large number of other regions, is that the issue of human rights treatment had not been factored in, at least not to the extent that restrictions were being imposed, or sales limited. Certain countries pressured by the U.S. to improve in the human rights area, including the countries of Brazil, Argentina, Uruguay, Guatemala, and Uruguay, rejected further U.S. aid, citing national dignity as the primary reason (Facts:171-172).

The authors of the book, Human Rights and U.S. Foreign Policy, Peter G. Brown and Douglas MacLean, go as far as stating the United States did not have an arms transfer policy (Brown:248). They state a vacuum existed in place of a clear-cut policy regarding common standards for review of a proposed recipient's stance. Because of this unclarity, inconsistencies are in abundance. National Security Advisor Brzezinski took time to explain the complex policy in a 1980 address to the chairman of the Eaton Corporation:

> The policy entails the sensitive balancing of its several components, which often conflict. The process can and does involve the occasional decision to forego a U.S. grant, loan or sale . . . In that sense, I could agree there is what you call a 'downside' to the human rights policy. But in fact the great majority of proposals are approved, either because they do not violate clearly established criteria, or fit clearly into an exception. (Dumbrell:188)

Chapter Summary

This chapter looked at the many intricacies behind President Carter's security assistance program, including:

- The evolution of the strategy during the presidential campaign;

- The passing of Presidential Directive 13 and the international reactions which ensued;

- Examination of the key components of the Carter implementation policy and strategy; and

- An analysis of exceptions to the human rights policy which undermined its consistency.

While chapter six will offer conclusions regarding the Carter attempts to increase global awareness of human rights issues, it is important to specify that there are always two sides to a coin. It is impossible to quantify improvements in human rights due to the policies employed by the Carter Administration. Flaws in the policy pertain more to the difficulty of generating a definition which can be applied universally, and a lack of consistency in applying the undefined requirement. The virtues of the policy are commendable by any standard.

V. Post-Carter Security Assistance Policies Under President Reagan

Chapter Overview

The objective of this chapter is to compare, contrast, and summarize the changes made to the United States Security Assistance Program when Ronald Reagan became the 40th President of the United States. The focus of this chapter is on the transitional changes accomplished when Reagan took office, and is not meant to be an affirmation or critique of the Reagan policies.

The Reagan Response

In contrast to the anti-government mood by the American public when President Carter entered office, President Reagan assumed command at a time when respect for the United States was perhaps at an all-time low. On the heels of the Iran hostage crisis, staggering inflation within the U.S. economy, the weak American reaction to the invasion of Afghanistan by the Soviets and the breakdown of SALT talks, the American public was enthusiastic and ready for the charismatic approach provided by President Reagan.

One of his first actions was to quickly discard Presidential Directive 13 by Carter which was originally established to restrict the sale of arms to countries based on humanitarian concerns. By rejecting the Carter philosophy, Reagan planned to use arms transfers to more effectively confront and counter the Soviet Union while also helping big business (U.S. weapons:3). Reagan officials boasted the effects of the arms sales would be substantial. Along with the tremendous boost to the defense industry, the U.S. Gross National Product would rise; U.S. balance of payments would improve; jobs would be generated; and the per unit cost of producing weapon systems would decrease, helping the Pentagon recoup research and development expenditures (U.S. weapons:3). Comparing the dramatic contrast between the Carter and Reagan arms transfer philosophies (Hutchins:11, 17):

Carter	Reagan
Dollar volume of commitments purportedly reduced[1].	No ceiling
Advanced weapons systems would not be introduced into a region until they were operationally deployed with US forces.	No restrictions.
Human rights within recipient countries and the economic impact were to be strongly considered prior to any arms transfer.	US national interests first.
Development or modifications of advance weapons for export	No such prohibition.
The burden of persuasion for arms transfers lay with the proponents not the opponents.	No such requirement.
US government employees were forbidden to help arms salesman abroad without specific permission.	Rescinded Carter directive.
An attempt would be made to reduce international arms traffic.	Arms sales not dependent on worldwide reduction--flexibility.

Table 5-1. Carter/Reagan Comparison

While giving his administration's Conventional Arms Transfer Policy Statement, President Reagan stated that the United States will only transfer arms in order to:

- Reinforce military capabilities to assist in the deterrence of aggression, especially from the USSR and its surrogates, and reduce the requirement for direct U.S. involvement in regional conflict.

---

[1] In actuality, no ceiling existed because of the innumerable exceptions and loopholes factored into the final totals.

- Reinforce the perception of friends and allies that the U.S. as a partner, is also a reliable supplier with a measurable and enduring stake in the security of the recipient country.

- Point out to potential enemies that the U.S. will not abandon its allies or friends or allow them to be militarily disadvantaged.

- Improve the American economy by assuring a more stable defense production base, and by enhancing the balance of payments. However, this objective should not be construed that the approval of the transfer of arms will be based solely on economic considerations and gains.

- Enhance the effectiveness of the U.S. military through improved possibilities of access to regional bases, ports, or facilities needed for the support of deployed forces during contingencies. Further, security assistance should be such as to improve the ability of the host nations to complement the U.S. forces during deployments.

- Strengthen the stability of a region and the internal security of the countries therein by fostering a sense of a recipient nation's security and thereby its willingness to settle disputes amicably. Through this objective, it is held that a government which feels secure is more likely to cope with such challenge in a more progressive and enlightened manner. (DISAM:1-31)

Most importantly, President Reagan issued a statement which provided the essence of his policy and highlighted the difference between his policy and that of the Carter Administration (DISAM:1-32):

> The realties of today's world demand that we pursue a sober, responsible, and balanced arms transfer policy, a policy that will advance our national security interests and those of the free world. Both in addressing decisions as to specific transfers and opportunities for restraint among producers, we will be guided by principle as well as practical necessity. We will deal with the world as it is, rather than as we would like it to be. We cannot play innocents abroad in a world that is not innocent. Nor can we be passive when freedom is under siege. Without resources, diplomacy cannot succeed. Our security assistance programs help friendly governments defend themselves, and give them confidence to work for peace. . . . Dollar for dollar security assistance contributes as much to global security as our own defense budget.

Along with the eloquent statement provided by President Reagan during his "State of the Union Address" before a Joint Session of Congress on 6 February 1985, President Reagan further berated the Carter policies in an extract from a statement by William Schneider, Jr., Undersecretary of State for Security Assistance, Science and Technology before the Committee on Foreign Affairs of the House of Representatives, March 3, 1983.

With respect to arms transfers and arms transfer policy, I would merely reiterate what many officials of this Administration have said before: We consider arms transfers to be an instrument of U.S. policy, not an exceptional instrument as our predecessors tried but in fact failed to establish, nor as a largely commercial activity as is the case with a number of other nations. We will continue to weigh carefully all of the relevant considerations likely to bear upon any specific arms transfer decision in order to determine whether the transfer is, on balance, in the clear U.S. national interest. These considerations include, of course, the military purpose of the proposed transfer, the ability of the recipient to absorb and operate the equipment, the economic impact of the proposed transfer upon the recipient, the impact upon surrounding states--stabilizing or destabilizing in the region and so on. As a practical matter, we continue to turn down proposed sales at a rate not significantly lower than our predecessors. This approach, we firmly believe, is sensible and ensures that arms transfers are integrated effectively with other instruments of policy and contribute to our broader strategic objectives.

Arms transfers are inherently neither good nor evil. Arbitrary restraint and unrestricted transfers are equally unrelated to U.S. national interests. There is no virtue in cutting arms transfers, or increasing them in the aggregate.

Sometimes there are clear and easy choices, i.e., approval or disapproval is unambiguously in the U.S. interest. In other cases, there are valid pros and cons. We must then decide whether, on balance, a proposed transfer is in the U.S. interest. We consult with the Congress, both to factor your advice into the decision-making process and to acquaint you with the factors bearing on the case, to sensitize you to the gray areas, and to minimize potential differences if we approve a sale and transmit it to you pursuant to section 36(b) of the AECA.

We also give close scrutiny to transfers of systems that incorporate advanced or sensitive technology. We must be assured that such technology will be adequately protected. This factor adds complexity to our analysis, because we must take into account the potential stability of recipient governments over the lifetime of the equipment being sold. The probability that a country will continue to share common policy objectives with us over the long haul is an important consideration as well.

Arms transfers are not substitutes for other forms of diplomacy. They are not an alternative to a long-term coincidence of national security interests between the U.S. and another government. They cannot guarantee harmonious bilateral relationships when fundamental interests diverge.

This being said, as I stated earlier in my testimony, if we want reliable friends, we must be one ourselves. Countries who cast their lot with the United States must know that they can count on our support to meet their legitimate military needs. Failure to respond prudently and appropriately to these needs would seriously damage our credibility as a leader of the free world, would decrease the chances of U.S. forces having to be deployed in a crisis, and would jeopardize defense cooperation with countries which provide access and facilities to the U.S. military. Our ability to supply friendly nations with appropriate arms contributes to a reduction in what would be larger U.S. defense needs to meet our national security objectives. (Schneider)

What was the attitude concerning human rights under the new administration?

While we would first believe that human rights was ceremoniously discarded, this is far from the truth, as the next section will show.

Human Rights

Human rights in regards to security assistance, a controversial issue during the presidential campaign due to its uneven, inconsistent application, and eventual discard as a viable policy during the Carter Presidency, remained a central issue, albeit a completely restructured one, during the Reagan Administration. While the Carter Administration was determined in its attempts to change the attitudes, beliefs, and abusive treatment of human beings, the Reagan Administration took a different approach. The Reagan Administration agreed with its importance, but also recognized that in many countries, societal structures are a legacy of the past and have evolved over centuries of privilege and subjugation, land ownership and peonage, tradition and history, war, race, and religion, and cannot be easily altered in a short period of time (DISAM:1-40).

Specifically, as one of the major differences between his administration and that of his predecessor, President Reagan spoke of the importance of defining violations of human rights caused by aggression and that of oppression. During the early forming of his human rights policy, Reagan recognized the difficulty in dealing with human rights violations caused by oppression. While the Carter Administration looked at violations under one scope, specifically the "effect," the Reagan Administration wisely included the cause of the violation. In reference to further repressive acts by governments in response to U.S. pressure, Reagan said, "It does little good to remedy the grievances of a few if that brings down worse oppression on the many." The U.S. can advance human rights more effectively than before by the full integration of human rights efforts into our diplomacy, pride in our achievements, and defense of our positions" (DISAM:1-40).

Chapter Summary

The purpose of this chapter was to provide a glimpse of the philosophical differences between the Carter Administration with those of his successor, Ronald Reagan. The comparison is intended on showcasing national attitude and the individual leadership styles of the two President's at the beginning of the Reagan tenure. While the two presidents had opposing views to a multitude of arms transfer and human rights issues, as evidenced in table 5-1 of this chapter, there were also similarities within their approaches:

1. Both Presidents ultimately viewed human rights as being subordinate to national/security interests in the context of broad foreign policy interests.

2. Both administrations were influenced by congressional intervention in the form of legislation and pressure to act.

3. President Reagan, and President Carter late in his administration achieved an awareness that both quiet and open diplomacy were needed. Both also understood the importance behind meticulously scrutinizing human rights practices of other countries prior to launching a crusade (Mower:153).

What were the underlying differences between the two President's? The most obvious difference was their approach to an escalating tension between the United States and the Soviet Union. Where Carter was hesitant and preferred a relatively passive approach, President Reagan entered the highest office prepared to counter Soviet action's with aggressive responses. Another recognizable difference was in the rhetoric put forth concerning human rights issues. Even though President Carter had all but dumped his human rights agenda in the latter stages of 1979, President Reagan still took it upon himself to lambaste the Carter strategy, saying, "We will deal with the world as it is, rather than as we would like it to be (DISAM:1-32)." This strategy, announced during a period of decline for the United States global image, was received well by an American public wanting to lift the demons of Vietnam, Watergate, and the botched hostage crisis in Iran. The Reagan approach also boded well for the U.S. military and the defense industry.

VI. Conclusions

Chapter Overview

At the beginning of this security assistance research, I started with preconceived ideas, expectations, and perhaps prejudices. I had preconceived ideas regarding the "weakness" of the Carter Presidency because of double-digit inflation, the slumping dollar, the Iranian hostage crisis, which in fact held the presidency hostage for 444 days, the botched rescue attempt of those same hostages, and what I felt was a serious decline of respect for the United States during his presidency. While I did not hold the Carter Administration in high esteem, this did not bias my research on the Carter Administration Security Assistance Program. I still expected to find a well-organized plan behind their global crusade for human rights. I also expected to find the human rights ideals were understood and consistently applied by the vast majority of the Carter team, even though admittedly, as will be discussed later in this chapter, it appears to be somewhat unrealistic to apply one set of rules to all countries.

While my research reaffirmed my overall opinion of the Carter Administration, I was very surprised to the degree that the Carter team did not fully understand the goals, ideals, and implementation policies of the human rights plan. This undoubtedly contributed to the inconsistent application of the policy.

Expectations aside, the purpose of the chapter is to review and analyze the accomplishments of the Carter Administration in increasing world awareness for human rights, whether the policy was understood and implemented consistently by the Carter team, and how Presidential Directive 13 fared in reducing the proliferation of arms.

Analytical Limitations

Prior to presenting analysis on the Carter performance in the area of human rights, one must understand the enormous difficulty and inherent complexity in critiquing human rights policies, of countries whose traditions, customs, values, and norms are dramatically different than those of the United States. These problems include[1]:

Positives gleaned from the policy are often difficult to quantify because of the reluctance of targeted countries to concede that United States pressure brought about the change.

Selected countries may have proactively modified their behavior prior to targeting so that sanctions would not commence.

Human rights are intangible, therefore we cannot quantify what we can't see. It is possible any of a number of human rights abuses would/could have occurred if not for the increased scrutiny of human rights issues by the Carter Administration.

Despite these restrictions, my research did uncover the tenets of the human rights policy and the problems and successes achieved by the Carter Administration.

Evaluation - Global Awareness for Human Rights?

Beset by the tragic experiences in Vietnam, stung by the shock, embarrassment and shame from the abuse of Executive power during Watergate, surrounded by economic woes and floundering with loss of credibility and respect around the globe, the United States faced one of the most difficult transition periods in its 200 year history in 1976.

Capturing the psyche of an American public favoring change, James Earl Carter was elected as the 39th President of the United States and promised a plethora of changes within the Executive Branch. One of those changes, the linking of human rights considerations to arms sales, serves as the basis for this thesis.

---

[1] This researcher's perspective.

Prior to speaking about faults within the human rights section of the Carter security assistance program, it is important to list the positive aspects of the policy. While it is easy to find fault with the human rights policy because of its inherent complexities and eventual discard as a valid tool as early as 1979, the human rights policy did elicit freedom for many around the world who would have otherwise remained prisoners within their own countries. According to Carter's National Security Advisor, Zbigniew Brzezinski, the Peruvian government released over 300 prisoners in April 1977; "disappearances" in Argentina " dropped from the thousands to 500 in 1978, 44 in 1979, and even lower in 1980; "disappearances" in Chile ended and most political prisoners were released; improvements were reputed to have taken place in Peru, Ecuador, Southeast Asia, and Indonesia; and in Indonesia, it was estimated that between an eight month period in 1977-78, more than 15,000 political prisoners were released and within the next two years more than 20,000 others were freed. The African governments of Guinea, Niger, Rwanda, Swaziland, and the Sudan also followed suit by releasing prisoners (Brzezinski:128-29). The administration also terminated security assistance to Bolivia, El Salvador, Guatemala, Haiti, Nicaragua, Paraguay, and Uruguay, and cut aid in at least one year to Indonesia, Tunisia, South Korea, Ethiopia, the Central African Empire, Guinea, Chile, the Philippines, and Thailand (Dumbrell:191). As a reward for improvements, assistance levels were increased in the countries of Sri Lanka, Botswana, the Gambia, Costa Rica, the Dominican Republic, and Peru (Dumbrell:191). On the punitive side, the administration banned the export of all equipment to the South African police and military, and used quiet diplomacy to dissuade the Dominican Republic from aborting election results (Dumbrell:191). Quiet diplomacy was also employed to obtain the release of fourteen political prisoners from South Korea (Dumbrell:191). Additionally, the following table suggests the Carter human

In each case, the table shows the number of stories on human rights jumped measurably from 1976 to 1977, and although the coverage did decrease after 1977, the amount of coverage still exceeded that prior to the Carter Presidency.

Additionally, during the Carter Presidency the United States took a more active role in the United Nations' human rights committee, and key human rights agreements were signed, including, the American Convention on Human Rights and the International Covenant on Civil and Political Rights and the International Covenant on Economic and Social Rights (Brown:12). On behalf of his performance, the International League for Human Rights cited that 1978 was a banner year for changes to human rights policies.

> First, within the past year, human rights has for the first time become a subject of national policy debate in many countries.
>
> Second, human rights concerns have also been the focus of greater discussion in international organizations such as the United Nations, the Organization of American States and the Belgrade Conference.
>
> Third, the world media has focused on international human rights issues to a greater extent than ever before.
>
> Fourth, consciousness of human rights among the peoples of the world has increased significantly.
>
> Fifth, there has been an easing of repression in a substantial number of cases. (Brown:13)

What were the problems with the human rights policy? Its proponents argue that it contributed to improvements in human rights in a number of countries, had a lasting effect on the media and its interpretation of human rights considerations, and impacted the organizational structure and decision-making apparatus of the Department of State (Vasquez:114). While these assertions may be true to a large extent, and it appears through my vast readings that the Carter directive at a minimum did raise the level of concern for human rights, there were some underlying problems with the Carter strategy.

Critics point to the uneven and inconsistent pattern in applying the policy, the confusion and lack of resolve which ultimately surfaced within the Carter Administration in carrying out the policy, that those most vulnerable to the U.S. directive were friendly regimes, and finally that the plan would not reduce oppression but instead, would in the long-run create greater oppression.

One problem with the policy was that it was implemented prior to being succinctly defined. This could explain why six months after he took office, a reporter stated:

> . . . throughout our government, officials have been struggling to wrestle an idea into a policy. . . one foreign policy official recently told me (that) "No one knows what the policy is, yet it pervades everything we do." Another official, who has done a good deal of wrestling, told me, ". . . There's no question that human rights was stated as a principle before anyone thought about it operational terms as a concrete policy. (Drew:36)

An interview with a member of the National Security Council by Elizabeth Drew highlighted other problems which impacted the ability of the Carter Administration in carrying out its human rights agendas, and were indicative of the continual problem of defining an exact policy:

> We came out that some things are obvious and there is a lot of gray area, that you have to work in the gray area, but you need flexibility. Its pretty easy to say torture, political imprisonment, arbitrary murder violate human rights. Beyond that, you start getting into important political areas. Some say it begins at breakfast, it's having jobs. Then you get into arguments about trade-offs: liberty versus having a job . . .Even if you could establish a natural law of human rights-- and there is a bit of natural law--there are other considerations of value to us: a country whose security is at issue. (Drew:54)

Evaluation - Presidential Directive 13

Was Presidential Directive 13 effective in restricting the sale of weaponry to noncomplying Third World Countries? No, although sales from the U.S. to Third World Countries only rose from $6.9 billion to $7.9 billion between 1977 and 1980, the major Allies of France, West Germany, the U.K., and Italy did not follow suit. Sales from these four countries rose from $6.9 billion in 1977 to $12.3 billion in 1980 (Brzezinski:145). Sales from the USSR also rose considerably, going from $9.6 billion in 1977 to $14.9 billion in 1980 (Brzezinski:145).

Not only did Carter fail to convince others of the merit of his strategy, even his goals fell far short. For instance, his intent on reducing the volume of arms sales fell far short as the total value of sales increased from $12.1 billion in 1977 to $17.1 billion in 1980 (Hutchins:17). It was also perceived that, by refusing to sell advanced weaponry to friends, the United States lost influence[3] within those countries and forced the countries in question to seek weaponry and technology elsewhere.

By 1979, it appears President Carter understood the ineptness of his arms transfer and human rights policies. Not only did he abandon the prior "restrictiveness" of his security assistance program, but he used it as a serious bargaining chip in his negotiation with Egypt and Israel at the Camp David Peace Conference.

Final Analysis

Making international human rights a feature of his presidential campaign, Jimmy Carter spoke often of the pride he felt in being a Southerner and an American (Rubin:61). Left alone, this belief would not be a problem. However, when President Carter presented his views on human rights in a self righteous, moralistic manner, he failed to recognize that

---

[3] Influence, as an intangible, cannot be quantified.

other nations, similar to Georgia and the United States, also take great pride in their religious and/or national ideals (Rubin:61). He also underestimated the difficulty in applying his human rights policy against hundreds of countries differing in customs, traditions, and beliefs. White House staffer Lynn Daft illustrated the problems with implementing the Carter human rights plan in 1977:

> The trick, of course, is in defining a . . .'consistent pattern of gross violations of human rights' and, once defined and the countries identified, figuring out a way to deal with the 'hit list' diplomatically and constructively. (Dumbrell:119)

President Carter's policy of linking arms transfers to human rights issues, and the underlying principles behind Presidential Directive 13, while holding much merit because of their intended purpose, proved to be ineffective for a number of reasons:

1. Human rights cannot be universally defined due to differences in customs, traditions, and norms related to individual countries[4].

2. Attempts made to enforce the human rights policy were inconsistently applied and control mechanisms were loosely implemented.

3. Countries friendly to the U.S. did not follow the guidelines put forth by Presidential Directive 13 and the holes left by the U.S. absence were quickly filled in. Multilateral cooperation was critical for any meaningful reduction in worldwide arms transfers.

An article written by The New York Times, January 24, 1977 presents perhaps the best overall view concerning the problems associated with extending a human rights agenda as a tool of security assistance:

> Making human rights the chief, or even major, foreign policy determinant carries dangers. . . . International law forbids any state from interfering in the internal political, judicial and economic affairs of another. Fundamentally, the quality of

---

[4] Although there is an enormous amount of difficulty and controversy in defining human rights, many countries have signed the Universal Declaration of Human Rights in order to establish a foundation for debate on the subject. This foundation is not legally binding, however.

life in a political community should be determined by its own people. (N.Y. Times, January 24, 1977:editorial page)

References

Arkes, Hardley. <u>Bureaucracy, The Marshal Plan, and the National Interest</u>. Princeton NJ, Princeton University Press, 1972.

Boven, Theo C. Van. "The United Nations Commission on Human Rights and Violations of Human Rights and Fundamental Freedom." <u>Netherlands International Law Review</u>, Vol. XV, 1968.

Brown, Peter G., and Douglas MacLean. <u>Human Rights and U.S. Foreign Policy: Principles and Applications</u>. Center for Philosophy and Public Policy, University of Maryland. Lexington, Massachusetts, and Toronto: D.C. Heath and Company, 1979.

Brzezinski, Zbigniew. <u>Power and Principle</u>. New York: Farrar, Straus, Giroux, 1983.

Brzoska, Michael and Thomas Ohlson. <u>Arms Transfers to the Third World, 1971-85</u>. Stockholm International Peace Institute. New York: Oxford University Press, 1987.

Carter, Jimmy. <u>Why Not the Best</u>? Nashville: Broadman Press, 1975.

Catrina, Christian. <u>Arms Transfers and Dependence</u>. United Nations Institute for Disarmament Research. New York, Philadelphia, Washington DC and London, 1988.

Cooper, Donald R. And C. William Emory. <u>Business Research Methods</u>. Boston: Irwin, 1991.

Council of Europe, Collected Texts. <u>European Convention on Human Rights</u>, Strasbourg, 1977.

Curti, Merle and Lewis P. Todd. <u>Rise of the American Nation</u>. New York: Harcourt, Brace & World, Inc., 1969.

Dane, F. C. <u>Research Methods</u>. Pacific Grove, CA: Brook/Cole Publishing Company, 1990.

Defense Institute of Security Assistance Management. <u>The Management of Security Assistance</u>. Wright-Patterson AFB OH, sixth edition, 1985.

Divine, Robert A. The Johnson Years, Volume Two - Vietnam, the Environment, and Science. Lawrence: University Press of Kansas, 1987.

Drew, Elizabeth. "Reporter at Large: Human Rights." The New Yorker, July 18, 1977.

Dumbrell, John. The Carter Presidency: A Re-evaluation. Manchester, UK, and New York NY: Manchester University Press, 1993.

Edwards, David B. and Terry L. Meneley. The Shaping of the U.S. Security Assistance Program. Wright-Patterson AFB OH, 1993.

Facts on File. Human Rights & American Diplomacy: 1975-77. New York NY, 1977.

Feigl, Peter. "ASPR Changes Made to Assist Military Sales." Defense Industry Bulletin, May 1965.

Freedman, Lawrence. Britain and the Arms Trade. International Affairs. London, 1978.

Gordon, Weil. "The Evolution of the European Convention on Human Rights," American Journal of International Law, no. 57, 1963.

Graves, Ernest and Steven A. Hildreth. U.S. Security Assistance, The Political Process. Lexington MA: D.C. Heath and Co., 1985.

Hovey, Harold A. United States Military Assistance: A Study of Policies and Practices. New York: Frederick A. Praeger Publishers, 1965.

Hudson, Manley O. The Permanent Court of International Justice. New York: Macmillan, 1934.

Hutchins, John G., Roger P. Labrie and Edwin W.A. Peura. U.S. Arms Sales Policy: Background and Issues. Washington: American Enterprise Institute for Public Policy Research, 1982.

Joiner, Harry M. American Foreign Policy, The Kissinger Era. Huntsville AL: The Strode Publishers, Inc., 1977.

Labrie, Roger P. U.S. Arms Sales Policy Background and Issues. Washington: American Enterprise Institute for Public Policy Research, 1982.

Logan, Fred A. and Edwin W. Rider. The Background and an Analysis of the International Security Assistance and Arms Export Control Act of 1976. Masters thesis, Air Force Institute of Technology, Wright-Patterson AFB OH, 1977 (AD-A047280).

Maresca, John J. To Helsinki: The Conference on Security and Cooperation in Europe 1973-1975. North Carolina: Duke University Press, 1985.

Maynard, Edwin. "The Bureaucracy and Implementation of US Human Rights Policy," Human Rights Quarterly, no. 11, 1989.

McGaffey, D. C. "Policy and Practice: Human Rights in the Shah's Iran," in D. D. Newsom ed., The Diplomacy of Human Rights. Lanham: University Press of America, 1986.

Mower, Glen A. Human Rights and American Foreign Policy. New York: Greenwood, 1987.

Moynihan, Daniel. "The Politics of Human Rights," Commentary, Vol. 64, No. 2 (August 1977).

Mozden, Stanley W., Jr. Military Assistance Training Program: A Military Instrument of Foreign Policy. Masters thesis, Pittsburgh: University of Pittsburgh, 1964.

Muravchik, Joshua. The Uncertain Crusade: Jimmy Carter and the Dilemmas of Human Rights Policy. Maryland: Hamilton Press, 1986.

Nathan, James A. and James K. Oliver. United States Foreign Policy and World Order. Boston, and Toronto: Little, Brown and Company, 1985.

New York Times. Editorial. January 24, 1977.

Pierre, Andrew J. The Global Politics of Arms Sales. Princeton: Princeton University, 1982.

Pollis, Adamantia, and Peter Schwab. Human Rights: Cultural and Ideological Perspectives. New York NY: Praeger Publishers, 1979.

Report to Congress on Arms Transfer Policy, Pursuant to Sections 202(b) and 218 of the International Security Assistance and Arms Control Act of 1976 (May 1977).

Rozell, Mark J. The Press and the Presidency. Boulder & London: Westview Press, 1989.

Rubin, Barry M. and Elizabeth P. Spiro. Human Rights and U.S. Foreign Policy. Colorado: Westview Press, 1979.

Sampson, Anthony. The Arms Bazaar. London: Hodder and Stoughton, 1977.

Schlesinger Jr., Arthur. "Human Rights and the American Tradition." Foreign Affairs, Vol. 57, No. 3, 1977.

Schneider, William Jr. Statement before the Subcommittee on International Security and Scientific Affairs, House Foreign Affairs Committee, March 3, 1983.

Sherwin, Harvey G., and Edward J. Laurance. "Export Controls Over Direct Commercial Sales of Military and Strategic Goods and Technologies: Who's in Charge?" Boston College International and Comparative Law Review, Vol. 7, No. 2, 1984.

Shoemaker, Christopher C. The NSC Staff: Counseling the Council. Boulder: Westview, 1991.

Truman, Harry S. Memoirs by Harry S. Truman. Garden City NY: Doubleday & Company, 1956.

United States At Large. Laws and Current Resolutions Enacted During the Second Session of the Ninetieth Congress of the United States of America, 1968, Volume 82. Washington: GPO, 1969.

United States Congress, Committee on International Relations. United States Arms Transfer and Security Assistance Programs, prepared for the Subcommittee on Europe and the Middle East, 95th Congress, 2nd Session, by the Foreign Affairs and National Defense Division, Congressional Research Service, Library of Congress, Washington DC: U.S. GPO, 1978.

United States Congress, Congressional Budget Office. Budgetary Cost Savings to the Department of Defense Resulting From Foreign Military Sales, 1982.

United States Congress. Foreign Assistance Act of 1961. Public Law No. 87-195, 87th Congress, 1st Session; as reprinted in United States Statutes at Large, Vol. 75. Washington: GPO, 1962.

United States Congress. Foreign Assistance Act of 1974. Section 26, 22 USC 2370.

United States Congress. Foreign Military Sales Act. Public Law No. 90-629, 90th Congress, 2d Session; as reprinted in United States Statutes at Large, Vol. 82. Washington: GPO, 1969.

United States Congress, House of Representatives. Committee on Appropriations. Foreign Assistance and Related Agencies Appropriations for FY1978, Pt. 1, Hearings before the Subcommittee on Foreign Operations Appropriations, 95th Congress, 1st session, 1977, p. 760.

United States Congress, House of Representatives, Committee on House Administration. The Presidential Campaign 1976, Vol. 1, Pt. 1, Jimmy Carter (Washington DC: U.S.GPO, 1978).

United States Congress, House of Representatives. Miscellaneous Reports Volume 6. Washington: GPO, 1949.

United States Congress. International Security Assistance Act of 1979. Public Law 96-92. Washington: GPO, 1979.

United States Congress, Joint Committee. Legislation on Foreign Relations through 1976. Vol. I, Annual Authorizing Legislation and Related Documents. Joint Committee Print, 95th Congress, 1st Session, 1977. Washington: GPO, 1977.

United States Congress, Senate, Committee on Foreign Relations. International Security Assistance and Arms Export Control Act of 1976-1977. Senate Report No. 94-876, 94th Congress, 2d Session, 1976. Washington: GPO, 1976.

United States Congress, Senate. Miscellaneous Reports on Public Bills, Volume 4. Washington: GPO, 1961

"United States Weapons Exports Headed for Record Level." Defense Monitor. Washington: Center for Defense Information, Vol. XI, Number 3, 1982.

Valencia, Teodoro. "We Stand to Gain," Philippines Daily Express, February 17, 1977.

Vance, Cyrus. Interview on Face the Nation. Department of State Bulletin. March 21, 1977.

Vance, Cyrus. News Conference. January 31, 1977.

Vance, Cyrus. News Conference. Department of State Bulletin. March 28, 1977.

Vasquez, John. Evaluating U.S. Foreign Policy. Praeger Special Studies, New York NY, 1986.

Whelan, Joseph G. Human Rights in Soviet-American Relations. Issue Brief IB77031, Congressional Research Service, Library of Congress, Archived May 8, 1978.